D1028242

RAISING LAZARUS

A True Story of God's Miracles

DARLENE MARCUSSON

WESTBOW
PRESS®
A DIVISION OF THOMAS NELSON
& ZONDERVAN

WestBow Press books may be ordered through booksellers or by contacting:

WestBow Press
A Division of Thomas Nelson & Zondervan
1663 Liberty Drive
Bloomington, IN 47403
www.westbowpress.com
1 (866) 928-1240

ISBN: 978-1-5127-7453-5 (sc)
ISBN: 978-1-5127-7454-2 (hc)
ISBN: 978-1-5127-7452-8 (e)

Library of Congress Control Number: 2017901776

Print information available on the last page.

WestBow Press rev. date: 02/21/2017

This book is dedicated to the great God we serve, who makes all things possible, especially Lazarus House.

Contents

FOREWORD

I would like to invite you to go on an adventure with me. It's a miraculous adventure filled with unexpected surprises and delights, a little heartbreak, and an overwhelming sense of God's love and power. This is a true story, but one many people may find hard to believe. How could it be? And yet it was and still is. Come with me on this adventure and experience the full realization that nothing is too hard for God.

CHAPTER 1

AND SO IT BEGINS

God had been hunting and haunting me for months. "Something's coming—be ready" was all that he told me. I was forty-seven years old and had no idea what the "something" was. I knew it was God who was speaking to me because he had been speaking to me since I first gave my life to him when I was fifteen years old.

I was born in Chicago and placed in the "nursery" connected to Augustana Hospital. "Nursery" was a nice word for the orphanage. Had I not been white and apparently healthy, I wonder what would have happened to me. But because I was the "right" color and didn't appear to have any overt physical defects, I was placed with a family who lived on the southwest side of the city.

I don't know when or how my parents told me I was adopted, but they did a good job because I don't remember ever not knowing. When kids in the neighborhood teased me, it didn't really bother me because my being adopted was as much a fact of life as my hair color or address.

As a child growing up, our neighborhood was populated primarily by people of Eastern European ethnicity. As I began to approach my teens, the neighborhood began to shift to a decidedly Hispanic population. That didn't bother me at all; however, my Spanish wasn't very good, so I had trouble communicating. My parents solved the problem by sending me to a school on the other side of the city and by shopping at stores where English was still the spoken language.

As a child, I always wondered why I wasn't taken out of the orphanage and put someplace where there were ponies and swimming pools. Especially as racial tensions mounted and riots broke out in my neighborhood, I wondered why I couldn't live in a place where people took vacations to Disneyland and had garden parties around their pool.

My life didn't include Disneyland, but it did include long bus rides through the worst neighborhoods in the city to get to my school. My fellow passengers spoke and acted differently, and I found their cultures and languages interesting. My parents weren't very accepting of other cultures or races, and so I wasn't encouraged to make friendships with people of other races or cultures. I thought that was silly, and that feeling crossed over to something much stronger with the civil rights movement.

Dr. Martin Luther King lived about a mile from my house that summer while he was in Chicago. Though there were riots in our neighborhoods during which shopping areas were burned, I felt strongly that the civil rights movement was a cause for which I should take a stand, especially after I gave my life to Christ.

My fifteenth birthday was not a happy day. I had been "excused" from my high school on the south side of the city the previous semester, along with most of the students who attended that school and lived in neighborhoods that weren't very nice. Consequently, I was attending a new school on the North Side. Since my birthday is in September, and school had just started, I really didn't know anyone, and no one at school knew it was my birthday. My mother was in the hospital, which was a very common occurrence because of her severe diabetes. My sister (we were not blood related but were raised together as sisters) was no longer living at home due to her elopement a few months prior. She was young and did the best she could, but her abrupt departure left my family in a shambles. My father had retreated behind his newspaper—the safest place for someone who didn't want to deal with feelings.

That morning I got up to go to school, and my father said not a word to me—not unusual for him. I came home on the bus after school and cooked supper, which was something I had done often since I was about nine. My father came home from work and ate supper, again without a word. I had one friend left in the neighborhood, as most of the white people had moved away. I went to her house, and her family remembered it was my birthday. They didn't have a card or a cake, but they did wish me a happy birthday—something no one else had done all day. I stayed at her house until around ten o'clock that evening.

When I got home, my father started yelling at me, asking where I had been and why I came home so late. I yelled back—I was a tough kid, and you had to be to survive my neighborhood and my family. I told him that I was at my friend's house and that at least they remembered it was my birthday. It was then that he said the thing that hurt the most: "Well, I remembered it was your birthday." I had to get my head around the fact that he hadn't forgotten; he just didn't care.

My father grew up with a series of losses. He was a child during the Great Depression in the 1930s. His family owned a small grocery store, and they lost it due to the faltering economy. He doted on his younger sister, who had a heart condition. She died in his arms at school after her heart gave out when she went up a flight of stairs. His older brother died when he was in his thirties, in large part because he staunchly refused to seek medical care. When my father's father died, my father was left to care for his mother.

When my father met and married my mother, I think he felt that this would give him a family and some security. My mother lived with her mother in a house that was purchased with the money they received from the City of Chicago when my mother's father was gunned down by a gangster. My mother's father was a

Chicago police officer, and in the 1920s many of them were killed by gangsters. The money they received enabled them to buy a two-flat, a signature Chicago two-story building with an apartment on each floor. They lived on the first floor and rented the second floor to tenants, which assured them a monthly revenue stream.

My father met with disappointment again when he and my mother found out that it was not possible for them to have children due to my mother's severe diabetes. Because my mother's health was so compromised, she battled with a series of health crises, and it was heartbreaking to see someone you love suffer so. It seemed to my father that everything he loved or hoped for had been taken away, and the best way to cope with all this was to shut himself off emotionally. It hurt too much to care, so he simply wouldn't allow himself to do that. My mother and father did the very best they could, but due to chronic illness and life disappointments, they were wounded.

The night of my fifteenth birthday, it became clear that my father could not give me what I needed from him emotionally, and he never would. To protect myself emotionally, I needed to stop expecting that he would. But how could I possibly grow up without a father's emotional support? Then I remembered what I had been taught in Sunday school.

My parents were "Christeasters," which is a term used to describe people who go to church on Christmas and Easter. However, they sent me to Sunday school when I was a little girl. I remembered what they taught me in Sunday school: that Jesus loved me no matter what. The concept of anyone loving me no matter what was very appealing, so I decided then and there that Jesus was what I needed.

All by myself in my living room in the dark, I asked Jesus into my heart—and the most amazing thing happened: he talked to me! He told me, "If you want to be different, you have to do different." Now, I didn't know what that meant, but I remembered what I had learned in Sunday school about this guy Jesus who went around helping people rather than punching them in the eye—something I was inclined to do often! So I decided I should look around for an opportunity to help someone.

There was a YWCA not too far from my house, and they had a program to help children learn how to read better. I didn't have too many talents of which I was aware, but I could read, so I decided I should start by helping at this program. That was my beginning of "being by doing."

Now, let me be clear here: we are *not* saved by what we do. Jesus did all that work for us on the cross, and his gift of salvation is free with no strings attached if we just believe. But as it says in the book of James, "What good is it my brothers and sisters, if you claim to have faith but have no deeds? Suppose you see a brother or sister is without clothes and daily food. If one of you says to him 'Go, I wish you well; keep warm and well fed,' but does nothing about his physical needs, what good is that? In the same way, faith by itself, if it is not accompanied by action, is dead" (James 2:14–16 NIV).

My time at the YWCA was most instructive. I learned that gangs were recruiting at the site, and the social worker in charge of the program—who I thought could walk on water—had his own agenda. The leader of the street gang in charge of the neighborhood stopped me in the hallway at the YWCA and peppered me with questions one day. I was the only white person volunteering at this program, and so suspicions were raised. I had no idea who this man was or why he was asking me so many questions, but I answered them honestly, and he finally walked away. I didn't think any more of it, and it wasn't until much later that I learned who he was and that he had put word on the street that no one should harm me. I am probably one of the few people who was kept safe by a street gang in the 1960s. But then, of course, Jesus was my real savior, and he sent his angels to have charge over me.

After high school, I attended the University of Illinois at Chicago, commonly known as UIC. It was 1966, and the suburban kids had discovered drugs. The Students for a Democratic Society was actively recruiting on campus, telling everyone how wrong the Vietnam War was and that we needed to stop this travesty. I certainly agreed that the war was wrong, but the methods that were being advocated were even more wrong, and I felt sorry for the students who weren't streetwise enough to understand what they were getting themselves into. My concern was confirmed a couple of years later when the students rioted during the Democratic National Convention in Chicago, and many students were beaten and badly hurt by police. I was outside SDS headquarters the first night of the riot and saw bloody, unconscious kids being carried in. They were too afraid to take them to a hospital because the police were staking out all the emergency rooms, so people with limited medical training were doing what they could to treat the wounded. The war was wrong, but this was not the way to make the point.

I felt increasingly uncomfortable at school, and then Jesus sent me the best gift I ever received (next to my salvation): my husband. He came wrapped up as a present on my eighteenth birthday, September 17, 1966. A high school friend was dating a man who was a few years older, but his birthday was on the same day as mine. Jerry gave us a party at his home on the north side of the city, and one of the people he invited was his colleague from work. That's how I met my husband.

We dated for a couple of months, and we both knew this was "it." Sam asked me to marry him in November, and we told our parents on Thanksgiving about our plans. His mother was very sweet but quite concerned because I wasn't from the right church (she belonged to a very legalistic church and felt that unless you worshipped at her church, you were doing it wrong). I think my parents were glad to have me off their hands. My mother unkindly told me the day after we announced our engagement, "You might as well marry him; I don't think you can do any better." In retrospect, I know my mother was entirely correct! My father, in his traditional fashion, had nothing to say.

I withdrew from school and got a job downtown doing something unheard of: processing income tax returns by computer. The office building was at Wabash and Monroe, and they had to reinforce the floors to accommodate the computers we needed to use, lest they plummet eight floors to oblivion. I am sure the desktop computer I am using at my home is more powerful than those computers were, as technology has advanced at the speed of light in my lifetime.

Sam and I were married on April 22, 1967, in a Lutheran Church on the north side of the city. We moved into a three-room apartment on the north side and began our life as young marrieds. We didn't have much, especially back in the days when no one bought anything except a car or a house unless they could pay cash for it. But we had each other and the Lord, so we were doing just fine. We were involved at the church in which we were married and worked with the youth, which was a perfect fit because we were youth too! We constantly saw kids involved with drugs and thought it was very sad; they had no idea what they were getting into. We also saw kids who related to God in a very contemporary way with music that was new and spoke to their hearts. It spoke to my heart too and still does.

Our first daughter was born in 1972, and we knew it was time to move out of the city. We didn't have much money, and housing was expensive, but we were determined to find a safe place to raise our daughter. The Lord prompted us to go to a town about forty miles west of the city, and while we were driving around the town, he pointed out some model homes tucked away in a corner. The minute we walked into one of the models, the Lord said, "This is your new home." He's done that for us every time we've bought a house, and he's never been wrong.

CHAPTER 2

A NEW BEGINNING

Living in St. Charles was a gift. I had never lived in a small town before and wasn't quite sure what to do when total strangers would speak to me on the street. We didn't know anyone and had no connections to the town, but we knew it was important to form some, so we did what God's people have done since apostolic times: we joined a church!

We found a church that walked the talk and was located about a mile from our house, which was a good thing, because we only had one car, and Sam took it to work every day. I was left with a baby and a bicycle, and that was just fine with me. I made friends in the neighborhood and at my church and went everywhere on my bicycle with my baby on the back. What great adventures we had, finding "secret" parks, visiting different libraries, and going to church almost daily for one thing or another.

My ladies church group visited the mental hospital in a neighboring town and the "boy's school," which was what they called the prison for juvenile offenders that was located in our town. I joined both efforts, thanking God for the opportunities to serve and for my experiences growing up that helped me be comfortable in settings that might cause others to run for the door. As much as possible, I included my young daughter in these efforts, knowing that it was imperative to preach the gospel at all times, and if necessary, use words.

One of the best service opportunities that came our way happened when the Vietnam war ended. Our church was asked to resettle a group of Vietnamese refugees, and my husband and I headed up the group that did this. My three-year-old daughter was with me every day of this effort and came to love our new friends, who spoke English about as well as she did. We all learned together and thanked God for putting this gift into our lives.

We loved our new life in St. Charles, but my husband's job was about an hour's commute one way, and it was wearing him down. We also were struggling financially, so we did two things: I took a part-time job as the welcome hostess for the chamber of commerce, and Sam took a job as a paid on-call firefighter. My position helped me get to know even more people in the community, and it also gave me a chance to help new people find needed services in their new community, such as a church or a doctor. Now who could have arranged that?

My husband enjoyed his work as a firefighter, and the town enjoyed having a caring, committed, capable man to rely on in times of trouble. They thought it would be good to be able to call on him at any time, day or night, so they offered him a full-time job working for our town, reasoning that if he was in town all the time, he would be available for emergencies day or night. Sam was delighted to take their offer and give up his arduous commute. And so we became even more entrenched in our town and continued to thank God for helping us have a new place to live that was a real home.

In May 1976 our second daughter was born. We were now a happy family of four, part of a growing community and a living church. We continued to serve at our church and in our community, and life was good but not perfect.

Sam was always a strong man, physically, spiritually, and emotionally, but he was getting worn down by all his physical activity. He had his first orthopedic surgery when he was twenty-five, and it was the first of many. In 1980 he had yet another surgery that kept him out of work for several months, so I rejoined the workforce in order to help pay the bills. I went to an employment agency in our community with a good reputation and explained that I would be available for a few months only. I was placed at a library system, and so began my next chapter.

I had always had a heart for the less fortunate, perhaps because I counted myself as one of them for so many years. My work at the library system put me directly in touch with these folks, as I was administering the Talking Books program for those who weren't able to access conventional printed material. These folks included those who were blind or legally blind, but it also included those whose physical disability prevented them from holding a book and those whose learning disability prevented them from deciphering what was written on the page. What a gift it was to be able to help these folks and make books available to them to give them hope and help as well as learning and entertainment. My temporary position developed into six years of serving in a way I loved. I went back to school and got a degree in library science and thought I would spend the next fifty years of my life in this capacity, and then God spoke to me again, and everything changed.

Our family had become part of a mission church in the mid-1980s. Ever since I first heard of this church starting in our community, I felt drawn to it. We had a home in the church to which we belonged, however, so I ignored God's urging to check out this new church.

Christmas Eve 1986 was a Christmas Eve none of us will ever forget. It was twenty below zero (actual temperature, not wind chill factor) and it was snowing sideways! Our church decided to cancel Christmas Eve services, about which I strongly disagreed. We had not been seeing eye to eye ever since they refused my offer to install a handicapped ramp without cost to them, enabling some of our physically challenged parishioners to attend church without physical barriers. Now they were closing the doors to everyone on Christmas.

Earlier that week we had received a mailing from the mission church God had been prompting me to check out, inviting the community to worship on Christmas. The mailing listed all the churches in the community and their worship times. I was very impressed that a start-up church that didn't have a building would spend money to invite people to worship at a church of their choice, and I wrote a note to the new pastor telling him what a great idea I thought this was. His note back to me came in the mail a few minutes after the phone call telling me that my church was canceling Christmas worship.

I need to admit that I am so stubborn that God has to literally shut the doors of my church and send me a written personal invitation to another church to get me to do what I should. That night we attended the mission church, and we knew immediately that this was to be our new church home. We embraced our new church and brought our passion for service along with us.

We loved our new church and were happy seeing it grow and serve. And then God spoke to me again. This time it was when I went out to my car and saw my neighbor across the street stuffing an obscene amount of groceries into her car. I called across the street to her, "Hey, Nancy, you think you've got enough?" Her reply was to change my life. She said, "Oh, this isn't for me; it's for that new homeless shelter they just opened in Aurora." Immediately the Lord convicted me as if I'd been hit by lightning; I just had to go there as soon as possible.

I found out where it was located and drove there. I will never forget my impression upon walking through their doors for the first time: *I was home!* These were the people I'd grown up with. Oh, they had different names and different faces, but they were the same people, beaten down by poverty and lack of opportunity, with a poor education and even worse health care. Immediately all the things that happened to me growing up made perfect sense, and I couldn't stop thanking God that he didn't put me in a place with ponies and swimming pools but rather in a place that would help me understand what it was like to live in those desperate circumstances. Thanks be to God, I got it!

This shelter became my new passion, and I involved my church and as many other churches as I could. I was there at least once a week, bringing my family and my church family. I was drafted to serve on their board and so had the opportunity to see the inner workings of a homeless ministry. I learned so many important lessons, and I was grateful for each one. Little did I know that God was getting me ready for something even bigger.

CHAPTER 3

HERE AM I; SEND HER, SEND HER

I was doing God's work day and night. My position at the library put me in touch with a hurting world, and I was able to put them in touch with resources that ministered to them spiritually and emotionally. My work at church put me in touch with my servant's heart, and my work at the homeless shelter put me in touch with my spiritual self. I was able to balance all this with my family, and was grateful again and again that my job at the library allowed some flexibility so I could be available for my children. Then God spoke to me again, and everything changed.

Our church had a small staff, two, and one of them was leaving due to her husband's job transfer. I woke up one morning shortly after hearing the news of her eminent departure with the absolute knowledge that God wanted me to replace her. I laughed out loud at him. "Impossible," I told him. "My job is perfect for my family. We all sacrificed so I could go back to school and get a degree in library science, and now you want me to throw all that away to go work at the church? Don't I do enough for them already? Who will look after my disabled readers? How will I be able to have enough time to devote to my children if I'm on call at the church? This will never work!" And I made sure it didn't have a chance to work because I told no one about this and ignored God.

In short order, I learned that they had hired someone else from the congregation. I told God, "See, they didn't need me. They have this other person, and I'm sure she'll do just fine." Except she didn't, and it was a minor disaster. It became clear to everyone in short order that she just didn't have the gifts for this position. Of course she didn't; she wasn't supposed to have the job; I was. But I refused to go, so someone else stepped up, and now everything was a mess. Some people from the congregation blamed the pastor for not letting this woman go sooner because she was making a mess of just about everything she touched. Others blamed him when he did eventually let her go for firing someone who was one of our flock and who needed a job.

All this was my fault because I refused to do what God asked. I bear guilt for this to this day. I know God has forgiven me and I've tried hard to forgive myself, but this taught me two important lessons: (1) when the Lord says "go," you go—no arguments, no excuses, no delays; (2) if you disobey the Lord, you aren't the only one who may suffer the consequences. I told God that I would never again argue or delay if he told me to go. Little did I know the extent to which he was going to hold me to that promise.

I went to our pastor and confessed my sin. By this time he didn't want to hire anyone from the congregation ever again, and I sure didn't blame him. Yet, I was convicted that this was what I was supposed to do, so I gave him my resume and asked him to pray about it. He called me the next day, and I wasn't entirely happy. We met and agreed that I would take a week's vacation from my job at the library and work at the church. At the end of the week, we'd see where things stood.

I did not have a good week. I was used to my position at the library and knew it well. I understood how things worked and had the answer to any question because I had been there for years. Whenever you start a new position, you feel inept. You don't know how things are done or where things are kept. Additionally, we had the best computers and equipment at the library because we were a government program. Our mission church had equipment that was primarily cast-off donations that were worn out and antiquated.

At the end of the week, the pastor met with me and asked me what I thought. I told him frankly that I did not have a good week, but that it was still my belief that I was supposed to be there. He concurred with me and so it was decided that I would give my notice at the library and begin my new position at church as soon as possible. I took a cut in pay, an increase in hours, and left my position at the library six months short of being vested in a state pension. God doesn't want excuses; he wants workers.

And work I did. Our church continued to grow. We built a building and soon outgrew it. We put on one addition and then another. We called a second pastor, and with that a true disciple of the Lord entered my life. He looked kind of gawky and really young and wasn't the best preacher or teacher I ever encountered, but he lived and breathed service. There was no better person God could have put in my life to teach me how to serve and lead like Jesus than Pastor John.

One of the many things for which I was responsible at church was community outreach. The executive director of the homeless shelter on the north end of our county and I became friends. We lamented the fact that our county had no department of human services, and so the people that provided these services across our county had no way to regularly meet and communicate. The end result was that some services were being duplicated while other needs were going unmet. We thought that we should convene a monthly meeting of service providers and invite every social service agency and church active in providing social services to that meeting. Since our church was located in the middle of the county, I asked our pastor if it could be used for the meeting place. Our servant-pastor was only too happy to help.

We really thought that eventually this group would spur the development of a department of human services in our county, and we were both disappointed as two years went by without any apparent progress in that direction. I was really beginning to think that the whole idea of having this group meet monthly was an exercise in futility, and then someone who regularly attended the meeting brought a three sentence newspapers article to our meeting.

I began this true story by stating that God had been haunting and hunting me for months. I was growing increasingly impatient with him, begging him to let me know what it was he wanted of me.

I always tried to read the local paper every day with an eye to any information that related to social services. Someone brought a newspaper article to one of our monthly community meetings that was to change my life. I don't know how I missed this article; perhaps because it was so brief I overlooked it. I sure wasn't overlooking it now.

The article said that our town was considering passing an ordinance to make it illegal to be a vagrant. I understood the reasoning behind this immediately. As was the custom in most northern states, homeless shelters closed in the summer. The thinking was that it was critical to offer shelter in the winter so folks didn't freeze to death in the streets, but when the weather warmed up, it was okay to allow them to camp outside. I don't know about you, but I sure don't want to have to live outside, no matter how nice the weather.

The two shelters that served our county closed in the summer, and many people from our community stayed at one or the other of them. Since they had to find a place to stay outside in the summer, they reasoned they would go back to their hometown and sleep on familiar park benches.

Our city administration didn't understand why more and more people were populating our parks every summer. Of course they didn't understand; they didn't volunteer at one of our county's homeless shelters, so they didn't know that they closed in the summer. The person who had this information (that would be me) never bothered to share it with them!

With another summer approaching, the city knew they would be getting lots of complaints from citizens who weren't happy with the situation in the parks, and so they were going to try to remediate the situation by empowering the police to arrest these "campers."

I am sure the city did not wish to be unduly harsh, but they did not know who these people were (our neighbors) and just wanted to solve a problem. The police had no wish to actually arrest someone for camping in a park, but if there was an ordinance that forbade park camping, then the police could move people along and get them out of the parks under threat of arrest.

I understood all this in the speed of light (God's illumination), and I understood something else immediately: God told me that this is the task for which he had me waiting. He reminded me of Micah 6:8: "What does the Lord require of you? To act justly and to love mercy, and to walk humbly with your God" (NIV). I knew what the Lord was requiring of me: start a homeless shelter right in our town.

Over the years I have been blessed by hearing the Lord's voice several times, but never had he been this clear or this adamant. I was stunned but also relieved because I knew there was no way this idea was going to fly. While I knew I had to raise the issue, I also knew it would get buried quickly and forgotten about. But hey, I could tell the Lord that I tried; you can't expect miracles from a middle-class working woman. I'd forgotten that I serve a Lord who specializes in miracles, and all he was expecting of me was to show up and give it my best shot. He was more than able to do the rest.

My idea was to write a quiet letter to the city council, but the next thing that God told me was that I had to wait. *Wait!* I've been waiting all these months, and now you finally tell me what it is I've been waiting for, and you want me to wait some more? God can be absolutely infuriating!

I waited for two days. During this time, I brought the news to my husband and my pastor about what God had charged me to do. Please keep in mind that the mayor was my husband's boss, and the mayor was in charge of the city council. I've always been told not to poke the bear with a stick, and I knew that telling the council they were wrong about this ordinance, even in a nice way, might mean that things did not go well for my husband or his employment. I also knew that many people in our community would not like this idea and get upset with me and the church I served.

My husband listened to me patiently while I told him what had happened, and his immediate response was, "Honey, I don't want you to worry. If God is telling you to do this, then you had better do it. We need to trust that God will work out the details." I told you he was a gift.

Next I told my servant-pastor what God was requiring of me. He was not naïve about the heat this could bring on our church, but he thought much more of the Lord than he did of public opinion. He too encouraged me to do what the Lord required and trust God to work out the details.

On Friday night of that week it was my church's turn to volunteer at the homeless shelter on the south end of our county. It was kind of a wild and wooly night there, and I didn't get home until the wee hours. I hadn't had a chance to read the local paper that day, and so it wasn't until about 3:00 a.m. on Saturday that I learned that the vagrancy ordinance was to be heard that Monday night.

Are you kidding me? How am I supposed to write a letter and get it in front of anyone with such short notice? How can I have any chance of stopping this ordinance from passing? On that Saturday, I called someone who understood the workings of the city council, and they explained that the vagrancy ordinance had been put on the consent agenda.

Before city councils meet publicly, there is a meeting of their executive committee, and they put together the agenda for the upcoming meeting. In an effort to keep meetings to a reasonable time frame, they bundle together several items about which they have consensus, and put those items on the consent portion of the agenda. When they meet, they vote the entire consent portion of the agenda up or down in one fell swoop—no discussion, just a vote.

The only way to prevent that from happening is to call the mayor's office and ask to speak to the item on the consent agenda you wish to address. That's what I did that fateful Monday morning. That afternoon I sat at the computer, but God wrote a proposal to open a homeless shelter. He gave me the words and the scripture to use, and I did the typing.

That night I went to my first city council meeting and sat in the audience waiting for the agenda item about the proposed vagrancy ordinance to be called. I knew only the mayor, and he was not smiling. A number of items of business were discussed, and then the vagrancy ordinance was brought forward. The mayor said there was someone who wished to speak to the issue, and it was God's turn to show up and show off.

I stood at the microphone facing the entire city council, whose members were ensconced in their chairs on a platform in a horseshoe around me. As I began to share the words the Lord had given me, a most amazing thing happened: I saw a ray of light much like a sunbeam begin at one end of the horseshoe and travel around to the other end. I finished my remarks; the mayor made a few of his own, which were not supportive or encouraging, and I sat down. I really wanted to leave the room, but knew I had to stay put until the end of the meeting. I couldn't wait to get home and warn my husband that the mayor may have a few choice words for him tomorrow. Little did I know what tomorrow would bring.

I had no idea that newspapers covered city council meetings. They do, and so the next morning when I got up, I was treated to three-inch headlines that read, "Proposal to open homeless shelter." Who could have thought that one very ordinary person making a few remarks at a meeting would have such impact? God knew, and that's why he told me to "wait." He wanted me in a time crunch so my idea of writing that quiet letter couldn't work.

He was obviously sending me as his messenger, and for once in my life, I didn't make excuses or try to run away. Whatever this meant or wherever it was going, I was in for the whole ride.

CHAPTER 4

THE WORK BEGINS

There was nowhere for me to hide. Lots of people in the community knew me through my work at church and in the community, and just about everyone knew where my church was, so I was easy to find. The phone started ringing, and I thought, "Oh boy, here we go, get out the tar and feathers." But everyone who called, and most of the people who called were people I did not know, said they thought this was a wonderful idea, and they wanted to know how they could help. I was stunned! Shame on me for assuming that people in my community were not concerned about the poor; they just needed a chance to understand the problem and a way to help.

One of the city council members called me the day after I spoke to the city council. I had never met the woman, and I did not know that she had been "assigned" by the council to make sure this thing didn't get too out of hand. I truly felt sorry for this woman, as I could hear the conflict in her voice. She knew this was the right thing to do, but she was concerned about what might happen. I didn't know it then, but God was sending a person who was to become one of our best supporters and a dear sister in Christ. He has sent so many blessings, and Betsy was one of the very best.

A few days later, another city council member called to say

that there was a meeting scheduled at city hall in a couple of weeks, and at it they had already planned to discuss some issues about unmet community needs. He suggested that this might be a good way to address the shelter issue and invited me to attend the meeting. Little did I know that his intent was to use this meeting to bury the issue, but the newspapers came to the rescue again. They learned of this meeting and made it front page news, forcing the meeting to turn into one that addressed the homeless shelter issue only and was open to the community. I could never have hoped to convene a meeting at city hall, but it was done for me.

As an aside, I want you to know that this city council member eventually not only changed his mind, but became one of our biggest supporters. And the city council itself passed a resolution we gave them approving the opening of a homeless shelter in our town. To our knowledge, that was precedent setting in the United States. Nothing is too hard for God.

At this point, I had no money, no equipment, no place, and no staff lined up. All I had was the Word of the Lord, but as I was to see, that would be enough. God does operate in the miraculous, but he often uses earthly resources to accomplish his purposes. If I was going to send the first funder for the shelter, I would have sent Oprah Winfrey or Michael Jordan, two very famous Chicagoans who had deep pockets. Instead, I got a call from a little girl I had never met. She went to another church in the community, and she was having her tenth birthday. She saw the article in the newspapers about the homeless shelter, so she decided to ask people to bring money for the homeless rather than gifts for her to her party. She wanted to know if it was okay to bring me the money. Little Katie brought her two hundred birthday dollars to me, and that was the beginning of our funding. When people heard about what Katie did, they felt moved to help too. After all, if a child can give up all her birthday presents, how could they refuse to donate something too? "And a little child shall lead them" (Isaiah 11:6, NIV).

Our first donor, Katie, today. She
is now on staff at a church.

The community meeting took place at city hall on a Saturday morning. Many people filed into the meeting room, and I didn't know any of them. I thought about the original *Frankenstein* movie when the villagers stormed the castle, and I was on the alert for pitchforks and torches. I was sure this meeting wasn't going to be pleasant, but I was an adult (or so I told myself), and I could handle some time on the hot seat; it would all be over in a couple of hours.

Instead of suggesting I be burned at the stake, everyone who spoke said they thought this was a good idea, and they wanted to know how they could help. A woman in the front row said she had been working with some of the students at the high school, and they had already raised $1,000. God's angels are sometimes heavenly, and sometimes one is the owner of a software company named Lynn. Of course the newspapers were at the meeting too, and they made sure the meeting was well reported in our local papers.

Community support seemed to be growing, but now what? It appeared that I would actually have to make good on the plan to open a homeless shelter. I had $1,200, but I still had no place, equipment, or staff. How could this idea possibly come to fruition?

I got on the phone and began calling around to find a place to house a shelter for a few months. As soon as whomever I was talking to heard the purpose for which I wanted to rent the property, the person hung up on me faster than the speed of light. We were a "homeless" homeless shelter, and that would never work.

And then God's people stepped up, as they always do, and we were offered the use of a gym that the Salvation Army owned. It was out in the country and far from ideal, but it sure could work. We did have $1,200, and the shelter on the south end of the county was able to lend us mattresses and bedding, as the operators closed their doors in the summer, and those things would sit idle until the fall. We still didn't have any staff, but I had lots of people who said they wanted to help, so I figured if I organized the volunteers and acted as the chief volunteer, we could get this off the ground. Now all we needed was a name.

I knew the name really would be important. It had to be something that caused people to understand immediately the purpose of the mission, and it had to be something that was invitational to people in need and gave them hope. I had several good ideas, and I checked with the Boss (AKA God) to find out which one he preferred. Much to my surprise, he told me "Lazarus House."

I have always liked the story of Lazarus, Mary and Martha's brother from Bethany. Lazarus died, and Jesus came and raised him from the dead. It was a very spectacular miracle, and it was the one that got Jesus in the most trouble because it was so public. In fact, that miracle sealed the fate of Jesus, because the powers that be decided after this miracle that Jesus had to go; he was just too famous. But still, I thought my suggestions were better, and so we "argued" for two days. That is, I argued, but God just smiled.

After two days, God finally told me, "You've got the wrong Lazarus." Another Lazarus? Oh, that's right, there's a beggar in a parable in Luke. It's the only parable in which someone is mentioned by name. Lazarus is a man of faith, and he is laid at the rich man's gate. All Lazarus wants are the crumbs that fall from the rich man's table. He doesn't get them, and Lazarus dies and goes to heaven. The rich man dies too, but he ends up in hell. He sees Lazarus in heaven and asks if Lazarus can please bring him some water, because he is in agony in the flames of hell. He's told that's not possible. He then asks if Lazarus can please go to his five brothers and warn them; they are all rich too, and think they have everything they need, and therefore feel they have no need of God. He is told no, that his brothers have what we all have: the scriptures and the prophets, and they need to pay attention to them.

And then I got it. Lazarus House was being placed in our community to help our neighbors in need, *all* of our neighbors in need. It's easy to see someone being evicted and realize that they have need, but what about the person living in the twenty-four-room house? What needs could they possibly have? Think about the rich man in the parable. Now, let me be plain: there is no sin in being rich, and just because someone is rich does not mean they aren't going to heaven. But isn't it normally true that our faith grows exponentially in times of trial? So for those who appear to have all the comforts of life and never have a care about any need that can be met through an abundance of financial resources, is their faith always as strong as the person who is in a sinking lifeboat?

The Bible makes it clear that we have a responsibility to share with those who are less fortunate. Our society often puts some disclaimers on that and suggests that those who are less fortunate would usually be fine if only they would work harder and stop wasting their money. Unless you're well acquainted with the "less fortunate," it's easy to buy into that mind-set.

But once you come face to face with someone who is truly "down and out," once you get to know them as a person, and once you understand that Jesus loves them just as much as he loves you, attitudes can change. Having a homeless shelter in the midst of an affluent community, a homeless shelter that serves only the immediate community, gives those who are coming to drop off a gallon of milk an opportunity to meet their neighbors in need. The real surprise to them often is that they meet someone who was a genuine neighbor—someone who lived down the block or was a classmate or goes to their church or worked with them at the phone company. Who knew they were now homeless? Suddenly, it's not "those people" any longer but your neighbors, and they need help.

Who, if they saw their neighbor struggling to carry a sleeping child from their car into their home, wouldn't rush over to help open the door? Your neighbors are now struggling with their sleeping children, and they need a door opened to a home that they can walk into. Once folks got that, they usually couldn't do enough to get and keep that door open. As is always the case, when you help someone else, you are the one who is truly blessed. I realized that Lazarus House was the perfect name after all. I guess God does have better ideas than me!

CHAPTER 5

THE DOOR OPENS

I always admired those people on the *Ed Sullivan Show* who would spin plates on sticks. They would carefully get first one plate balanced and spinning on the top of a long thin stick, and then they'd add another stick and plate, and another and another, all the time keeping the first plates spinning so they didn't crash to the ground and break. Now I was one of those people, running back and forth and juggling my family and my job at church and attending to all the details required to get the doors of a homeless shelter open.

I had a cadre of faithful volunteers who were willing to do whatever it took, and together we hauled mattresses and combed garage sales for important pieces of equipment such as coffee pots. My oldest daughter, Nicole, was in college and had elected to attend a small Christian college close to our home and become a commuter student. She had attended a large state university her freshman year, and found that living in a dorm and the entrapments of college life were not her cup of tea.

My family had always come with me to the homeless shelter on the south end of our county to volunteer, and shortly after Nicole made her decision to become a commuter student, a staff position opened there. At the age of nineteen, my daughter was offered the position of emergency shelter coordinator, which meant that she would be in charge of the overnight emergency shelter and work with church volunteers to keep things running smoothly. She eagerly accepted the challenge and stepped into the role with youthful enthusiasm and a heart for the Lord.

Her experience made her the perfect ministry partner for me when it came time to write out policies and procedures for Lazarus House. God is not lazy or slipshod, and he does not expect us to be either. Nicole and I spent many nights into the wee hours banging out policies and procedures and creating forms to use. God kept us on our toes and kept bringing to mind details that might have slipped by unnoticed. He is so faithful!

One of the details he was adamant about was the need to apply for a 501(c)(3) for Lazarus House. God's work does not need governmental recognition or approval, but that "Give to Caesar what is Caesar's, and to God what is God's" (Matthew 22:21, NIV) doesn't just apply to tax money. God expects us to work within the framework of our government, and so legitimizing a social service ministry by taking the steps necessary to make it an officially recognized charity was something he was requiring.

One of the best lessons Lazarus House taught me was that God will provide. I always believed that in an abstract sort of way, but there was nothing abstract about the needs of Lazarus House. Applying for a 501(c)(3) was a difficult and arduous task, one for which I had neither the time nor the experience.

It is said that God does not call the equipped; he equips the called. I found that I had many gifts of which I was not aware, and I wonder if I even had some of them before Lazarus House started. Corrie Ten Boom, the famous Holocaust survivor, tells a story that her father told her. Corrie was concerned because she was beginning an undertaking, and she didn't know if God was going to provide for all the needs. Her father asked her if she remembered the train trips she took to visit a relative when she was a child. He reminded her how he used to take her to the station and hand her the train ticket just as she was boarding the train. He asked her if she understood why he didn't give her the ticket any sooner. She responded that she imagined it was because she might lose it. Her father told her that was the correct answer, and so it was with gifts from God: they will show up just when we need them. God is never late, but he is seldom early.

When it wasn't possible for God to equip me for something (I am not suggesting that God has limitations, but I clearly have some), then he would send someone along who had just the gifts that were needed. This was true with my friend Bill.

Bill attended my church and was a little newer to that "Jesus thing." Bill was very smart, and his intellect was a faith challenge for him, as it is for many "thinkers." One day I was standing in the narthex at church by the sign-up poster for our monthly turn at the homeless shelter on the south end of the county, and Bill walked by. I literally reached out and grabbed his arm and reminded him he'd been telling me he wanted to volunteer at this shelter, so this was it! I really needed his help that month, and because I caught him off guard, he had no ready excuse and signed on the dotted line. It was to change his life.

The night Bill showed up at this shelter was an especially difficult one. It was more crowded than usual, and the weather had been horrible. People were stressed and scared, and many of the children were sick. It was a night to test anyone's faith. Bill and I stayed all night and drove back together in the morning. I'll never forget watching his face as the sun rose and seeing the tears in his eyes as he exclaimed over and over, "I just never understood; I just never understood." He understood now, and he was hooked! He just couldn't get enough of serving that Jesus he hadn't been so sure about.

I've said that Bill was an intellect, and that was true. The way God had used his intellectual capacity was to make him a lawyer! I could fill the page with lawyer jokes, but none of them would apply to Bill, as he was completely ethical and honest, and now he was going to put all that energy and expertise into serving Jesus.

I needed someone to help apply for a 501(c)(3). Bill was the guy! He tore into the project like a bargain hunter at a clearance sale. He warned me that it usually takes at least three months to get a response once the application is submitted, and he cautioned me to be patient (something at which I do not excel). Two weeks, that's all it took for the application to be received, favorably reviewed, and approved. Bill said this was unheard of, and he was flabbergasted. I told Bill that I knew he did good work, but that the real worker here was Jesus, and nothing was too hard for him. I told Bill that this was just one of the many miracles he was going to see, and I was not wrong.

June 6, 1997, is a day that will live in infamy for more than one reason. In addition to it being the anniversary of D-Day, it was also the day we opened the doors of Lazarus House. We had been terribly busy retrofitting the Salvation Army gym into usable space, collecting needed supplies, getting policies and procedures ready, and organizing volunteers. The newspapers kept the community alerted that we were actually going to open our doors and where we would be located, and so we were all ready. Except that I forgot to send out invitations to our guests. The actual date that the doors were opening was not published anywhere. One of our faithful volunteers and I spent the first night sleeping on mattresses on the floor of a homeless shelter without any guests!

The next morning, I got busy printing up flyers announcing our opening and alerting the newspapers too. That afternoon our first guest appeared. He came walking through the door of the gym, and the sun was shining brightly in back of him, causing a halo effect. That was not a coincidence, but rather what I call a Godincidence.

"Steve" was well known in our community. He was a burly man with long curly hair who struggled with mental health issues. His grandmother lived at a subsidized seniors' apartment complex in our community, and "Steve" would stay with her for a day here and there, but it was against the rules for him to live there. So he would float around, living in various shelters far from home, or in the woods when the weather permitted. But now there was a shelter in his town, the town in which he grew up and where his family lived, and he could get the care and help he needed there. What a gift to "Steve" and his family, and to us. That second night our volunteer and I slept on mattresses on the floor of the gym with our first guest, and he was to be the first of thousands.

Over the next few days, others showed up, including an eighteen-year-old woman who was nine months pregnant, and a man who had been living in a storage locker. I had heard about this man, "Willie" from the police, and they told me that unless he vacated the storage locker, they were going to have to arrest him. I took a friend with me and went looking for "Willie," locating him sitting in a lawn chair outside his storage unit/home. I told him that there was a shelter open in the community now and asked him if he wanted to come with me so that he would have a safe place to stay. He decided that sounded like a good idea, so he got a little suitcase and began to pack.

I've had a lot of experience with mental health and substance abuse issues in my life, most especially due to my extensive experience at the shelter on the south end of our county. Still, I realize now that I was poorly equipped to deal with the depth of these issues, and God was going to have to send me back to school for more training in order to make Lazarus House all he intended it to be. "Willie" was a prime example of my need for more training.

That night while our guests tried to sleep, "Willie" came to me in our little gym kitchen. He was in bad shape physically, shaking and sweating and telling me he didn't feel well. He also said he was having really bad dreams. I believe now I was witnessing delirium tremors (DTs), but I didn't know enough about them to recognize them. I asked "Willie" if he wanted me to call an ambulance, and he said he didn't. I immediately began praying and asking God for wisdom and guidance and protection for "Willie." I had my Bible on the kitchen table, and God prompted me to pick it up, and he began to give me scriptures that I was to read to "Willie."

I am a big fan of Bible study. It deepens your relationship with God, and it gives you tools to live by. It also gives you tools to bail the lifeboat when it's sinking. Anyone who knows about having tools available for emergencies knows that it's important to have the right tools nearby, keep them in good condition, and be well versed on how to use them. The worst time to have to hunt for a fire extinguisher is when the kitchen is in flames. So it is with his Word; be familiar with it and have it handy. Tuck little pieces of it away in your heart so you can quickly pull them out in an emergency and spring into action.

The scripture the Lord gave me for "Willie" that night spoke to him in a way I never could. After reading scripture for a while, I prayed with "Willie," and he was visibly improved. The shaking and sweating had stopped, and he was calm. He told me he thought he could sleep now, and that's just what he did. That made one of us! I was up all night praying and watching and making sure "Willie" was peacefully sleeping.

In those early days, I picked up our guests at the police station in town in my minivan and drove them to the gym/shelter, which was located a few miles out on the edge of town. That day when I picked up our guests, I ran into a pastor from our town who had been trying to help "Willie." He had heard that I found "Willie" in his storage locker/home and had taken him to Lazarus House. He thanked me for trying to help "Willie" and said that we shouldn't give up praying for him and trying to get him to go get some real help.

As the sun rose on a peacefully sleeping "Willie" that morning, I telephoned that pastor and told him what had transpired the night before. The pastor told me that the Lord had awakened him at 4:00 a.m. and that he had been on his knees ever since praying for "Willie." I was not the only one who had a prayerful, sleepless night, and I realized that this was how much God loved "Willie."

I asked the pastor for his recommendation for a place to take "Willie," and when "Willie" woke up, he immediately came to me and said he was ready. Just like that. I didn't have to sell the idea or beg or plead or try to reason with him; God had prepared the ground and covered it with prayer.

I called the pastor, who met us at the police station when I dropped everyone off in the morning, and he took "Willie" to a men's Christian treatment center. "Willie's" life here on earth may never be ideal, but it is much better than it was, and he also has the promise of eternal life because he knows his Lord and Savior better than many of us ever will. You see, "Willie" has had to depend on God for his very life every day. The fact is, we all do, but many of us don't recognize that fact. "Willie" acknowledges and celebrates his daily dependence on God; that's one of the best lessons I've learned from my brothers and sisters in desperate need.

CHAPTER 6

THE DOOR CLOSES

The summer of 1997 will always be the summer I remember as my summer of miracles. So many things happened that summer that caused me to fall to my knees in thanksgiving and praise! When our time at the Salvation Army gym was coming to a close, we needed a new home, and my church stepped up and offered its education wing.

My pastor lived and breathed service, so it was completely natural for him to help the church council see what a good idea it was for Lazarus House to have a home at our church. Never mind the fact that we were located in a very affluent part of town where the homes were more like starter castles; a homeless shelter was just the right fit.

Being at our church meant that we were still on the edge of town, and it was still necessary for me to pick up and drop off our guests at the police station, but we were all used to that routine, and it was working nicely. I reasoned that if someone didn't want to be in close proximity to the police station, then that was a person I really didn't think would be a good candidate for Lazarus House. Right from the beginning, the police were very supportive of our efforts. God's favor has always been abundant in and around Lazarus House, and this was just further evidence of that.

Among the new guests who came to us in July that year was "Bobby." My oldest daughter, Nicole, had gone to school and had been in the same class as "Bobby." He was always loud and somewhat out of control, and in trouble more often than not. When Nicole was in third grade, "Bobby" stole her bike, and she came home crying uncontrollably. Several kids had seen "Bobby" take the bike, so we knew who had it. My husband knew "Bobby's" stepfather, so Sam called him, and in short order the bicycle, minus the purple and white basket, showed up in our driveway. Since that time, Nicole had always feared "Bobby" and steered clear of him.

Nicole had volunteered to be the person in charge of Lazarus House one night that July, giving me a night off and some much-needed uninterrupted sleep. Who should come knocking on the door for the first time that night? "Bobby," of course. Nicole opened the door and was dumbstruck. The man at the door was "Bobby" without question, but rather than the ogre she had built up in her mind over the years, there was this small, sad, disheveled man who needed help. She was privileged to invite him in, and so began their celebration of renewed friendship. She came to know him as the funny, kind, lost soul who was in bondage to drugs and alcohol, and he came to know her as the wise, warm wonderful friend who would help him but also hold him accountable. Good to have friends like that.

I learned just this year that "Bobby" was found dead on the street. He was the apparent victim of a hit-and-run driver. His life was filled with struggles, but it was also filled with people who cared about him. He knew that he could always choose to be surrounded by God's love and God's people through a miracle named Lazarus House.

Another gift we received that July came in the form of a seventeen-year-old. A friend brought this teen to our door one night. The teen was very hungry and in desperate need of help. While this young person was in high school, her family moved to another state. This teen had never made friends easily, and this move was extremely difficult for her. She left her home and came back to her old "home," a community in which she felt the most acceptance and love she had ever experienced. Except she no longer had an actual home in our community, so she tried to find an old neighbor or friend who would take her in. One of those old friends brought the teen to us.

Now what were we to do? Obviously, we took her in immediately and gave her something to eat and offered clean clothes and a shower. But she was only seventeen, and, by law, we were not able to keep a minor with us without parental permission. The parents lived hundreds of miles away, and the teen didn't want us to call them, so the situation was complicated. I knew I could call child protective services, but they are overwhelmed and not too interested in dealing with the issues of someone who will be aging out of their system shortly.

As always, God was my best adviser, and he suggested I call my friend Bill, the attorney. I told Bill what was going on, and he said he would draw up a document that, if signed by the teen's parents, would enable us to keep her with us legally. I explained to the teen that we really wanted to help her and have her stay with us, but that I couldn't keep her legally unless we were able to get parental permission. By God's grace, she agreed that we could contact the parents, and, with his further grace, the parents were relieved to hear from us and learn that the teen was safe. Via fax, we got the documents sent to them, and they signed them, got them notarized and faxed them back to us. The teen stayed with us for about two weeks, and by God's grace we were able to help the teen see that returning to her parents was in her best interest. The parents were delighted to have their child back, and the teen was glad to be reunited with them. Thanks be to God!

Our time at our church came to a close, and we needed to find yet another home for our homeless shelter. Then the church I had belonged to for years when I first moved to St. Charles contacted me and said they would be willing to have us stay in their gym. What a gift! Rather than being located on the edge of town, they were located in the center of town, so our guests didn't have to depend on me to pick them up.

We were on the move again, but thanking God for the opportunity to be in the heart of town. Now, if you know anything about shelter ministries, you will know that in smaller towns, they are almost always located on the edge of town or in some industrial park—anywhere but the downtown area. So to say this location was unusual is quite an understatement. "Nothing is too hard for God" (Jeremiah 32:17, NIV).

Especially with this improved location, more and more of our neighbors in need found their way to our door. That first summer, fifty-two men, women, and children came to stay with us. They were all ages, and their stories were all different, but they all had one thing in common: they needed help, and God had placed Lazarus House in their midst "for such a time as this." For those in our community who said there was no need for a shelter, we now had fifty-two ways to show them they were wrong. For those who said a homeless shelter would cause nothing but problems, we now had a record of operating peacefully for months without problems or distress.

The original concept of Lazarus House was to provide shelter for our neighbors in need during the summer, when the shelters in neighboring communities closed. As the summer drew to a close, we began to prepare our guests for the transition. We explained that shelters in neighboring communities would be available for them, and we offered bus passes for those without cars, and tanks of gas for those with cars so they had a way to get to those shelters. But they were many miles away and not at all like the "homey" Lazarus House they were used to.

I was praying for God to help them have hope and not be afraid, and he said, "Ask them to dinner." And just like that I knew he meant Thanksgiving dinner. So I asked our guests what they were doing for Thanksgiving, and surprise! No one had any plans. I invited them to come back to Lazarus House for Thanksgiving dinner, telling them we would be open for just that occasion, and they were delighted. It gave them something to look forward to, and also gave them hope that we would be back in the spring. Little did I know just how "back" we would be!

Two days before we were getting ready to close our doors for the winter, a family showed up with a sick baby. They had taken the baby to the emergency room at our local hospital. The hospital staff had examined the baby and determined that she had an infection that required antibiotics. They gave the family a piece of paper that was to be used to cure the baby. The "paper" was a prescription that could be traded in for medicine at any pharmacy. Except that the family didn't have any money, and no pharmacy at that time was giving away medication. Didn't anyone realize that this family was homeless and had no way to get the medicine this baby needed? I learned that the truth is the family didn't tell the hospital staff that they were homeless and had no money for the medication. How could the hospital possibly know the situation? Yet another lesson learned in dealing with people in need: they are often embarrassed and won't tell anyone what they need. I called one of our stalwart volunteers, who immediately showed up and turned the "paper" into "magic" medicine that cured the baby's illness. I knew more must be done to help people with medical needs. Little did I know what God was going to do about that.

CHAPTER 7

THE WINTER OF OUR DISCONTENT

Saying good-bye to our guests and entrusting them to the care of shelters in neighboring communities was very hard, but it was also a relief. That summer had been filled with miracles and God's grace and an infusion of the Holy Spirit's energy that you can't explain to anyone who hasn't experienced it. Yet, it was hard to balance my family with my full-time job at church and my full-time work at the homeless shelter, so I was grateful to get back to a more normal life and sleeping at home in my own bed every night.

Autumn always brings Thanksgiving, and as I was praying about our Thanksgiving feast at Lazarus House, the Lord said, "It isn't enough," and I knew he meant I was to invite others to dinner as well. I was sure there were other people in the community who were going to be alone for Thanksgiving or couldn't afford a lavish feast, and sending them an invitation to dinner would be a welcome gift. So I crafted a very "elaborate" three-sentence press release inviting anyone in the community to come to our feast. I expected about twelve people.

I cooked two turkeys and made a pan of sweet potatoes and stuffing, thinking that would be enough to serve the few people that would attend the feast. Seventy people showed up! If you are familiar with the story of the loaves and the fish, then you will know what happened that day. Not only did we somehow have enough food for everyone at the feast, we had so many leftovers that I had to drive them around to the fire and police stations in our community, sharing our Thanksgiving bounty with them too. Until the day I traded that car in, I had cranberry stains on the roof because I literally had leftovers stacked from floor to ceiling that Thanksgiving Day. We serve a great God!

His greatness continued throughout that winter. While I was still sad that our guests had to be miles from home, I was looking forward to opening our doors in the spring. I was hopeful that we could find a suitable site, but again any phone calls I placed to available rental space were met with a firm *no*. Even though we had a good track record from the past year, it didn't help; no one would rent to us.

And then I received a call from a pastor in the community I had met once. He said his church had been praying about what to do with the extra space they had in the building they had recently acquired, and they felt led to offer it to Lazarus House. I was flabbergasted! I didn't know these folks, but I sure knew their building, and it was located in the heart of the downtown area. It would be an ideal place for Lazarus House.

I met with their church council, and we talked about conditions for our renting space. They offered a rental agreement that was extremely generous. They said they were hopeful we could help offset some of the utility expenses too, but if we couldn't, they would understand. Please know that this was a congregation that worshipped less than one hundred every Sunday and did not have large resources. Yet, they were directed by God to offer a homeless homeless shelter a home, and they obeyed, despite the fact that this could be expensive for them.

One of my favorite stories in the Bible is the story of the Annunciation (Luke 1:26–38). I've shared this story with many people over the years, telling them that I want to have a "Mary" heart, meaning that I want to respond to God's call as Mary did. You may remember that she was visited by an angel who told her she was to have a child, even though she was a teenager who was not married. In her time, that usually meant that her family would disown her and that the townspeople may stone her to death. Yet Mary's response to the angel's news was, "I am the Lord's servant; may it be with me as you have said." Clearly this church, although small in numbers, had a giant Mary heart.

Now that we were to have a permanent home, we needed to get it ready. We had little money and no expertise in renovations, so the Lord sent a man named Joe McMahon. He owned a construction company and was affiliated with the Remodelers Council and the Geneva Rotary Club. He contacted me out of the blue (by now I was used to getting calls "out of the blue," understanding that our Lord was the one who arranged them), saying that he wanted to help us in some way. Was there something he could do? God was right on time once again.

I met Joe at the church and showed him the space we had been allocated. Joe told me he would take care of everything, and he would do his best to get services and materials either donated or at very discounted prices. I was most grateful for this but also a bit nervous, because I wasn't given an actual estimate, and I knew our resources were very limited.

Joe began to work away, and I began to plan for our reopening that spring of 1998. We still didn't have any staff, and I knew I was in for another summer of little sleep, but it was really much worse than that. Since the church had offered us a permanent home, the Lord had told me that we had no excuse to be a seasonal shelter any longer, and that we now could be open year round. What a ridiculous idea! No emergency shelter in our part of the world was open year-round! How could I possibly offer a year-round shelter when we had no staff? Haven't I done enough! Are you never satisfied, Lord?

God responded by sending another miracle. In Illinois there

are things called Community Development Block Grants (CDBG). This is money that comes down from the federal government to the state government. The money can be used for many good purposes, such as road and bridge renovations, but one of the requirements is that some of this money must be used to fund homeless services.

The cities to the north and south of ours had been receiving CDBG money for years, as their populations were high enough to qualify them for this funding apart from the state. Our community, however, didn't have sufficient population, so the money was not sent our way. But then in 1997, our county decided to do a special census, the result of which showed that our population was now sufficient to qualify for these funds. Now let me think, when else in history was there a special census that fulfilled God's purposes? I seem to remember a homeless family that was wandering the streets of Bethlehem looking for a place to stay due to a special census. God took care of them too.

Since our county was now to be a recipient of these funds, they had to find a way to spend part of them on homeless services. As the shelters to the north and south of our community already received CDBG money through their cities, we were the only homeless services provider that could qualify for this money, making it possible for our county to claim all the CDGB funding that was available. God's wisdom in prompting me to apply for a 501(c)(3), and his provision of attorney Bill to get the application completed expertly so that it was approved immediately, again became clear.

The man who administered this funding for our county turned out to be a wonderful brother in Christ. He had to be ethical and fair and show no bias, and he was careful about all of those things. It gladdened his heart to see God working through all this.

He did ask for my help in one area. Part of the requirement to receive this funding was that the county set up a group of social service providers that would meet monthly to share information and collaborate. He wondered if I could possibly help get such a group started. I told him that not only could I help, I could hand him one that was already established and had been meeting for three years! All that time when I was wondering what real good those monthly meetings at our church of social service providers was doing, God knew how it would be used. It's imperative that we trust him and his timing. I contacted everyone in the group and told them that the next meeting would be at the county building, and so our county's Continuum of Care came to be.

We now had our first major grant of $25,000, and we could hire an actual staff person! As always, God sent his best: a brother in Christ who loved the Lord with all his heart and was also an ex-Army Ranger. Just the combination we needed! This man's wife was the woman who had stayed with me the very first night that Lazarus House opened, the night when no one showed up. So this family had been with us from the beginning and understood what the mission was about.

It seemed we had everything lined up to begin our next chapter: a permanent home, staff, and some of the equipment we needed, *some* being the operative word here. We had begged and borrowed many items, and for the most part we had the essentials covered, except for one very important item: a refrigerator. The one we had that was being stored in my garage during the winter of 1997 was a very small, old Westinghouse. I remembered those models from when I was a child, and it was impressive that it had lasted all these years. Except it was prone to leaks, and it wasn't large enough for the amount of food we needed to store. I was concerned that food would spoil, and people might become ill. We needed a large commercial refrigerator.

God promises to provide everything we really need, and we needed a refrigerator. I began to pray earnestly for one. I didn't feel that we could go out and buy one. Joe was working away at the renovations and, true to his word, was getting many supplies and labor donated. But he still couldn't put a price tag on the end result, so I had no real idea of what kind of money we would have after paying for the renovations.

I called restaurants in our community that had recently gone out of business, hoping for an outright donation or a very reasonable sale price, but I had no luck. I called around to get prices on a new commercial refrigerator, and even though I was happy with a "Chevy" rather than a "Cadillac," the price was still quite high. I was pretty upset with God for not providing for this need, and then he began to say to me, "Trust me."

Now it's just fine to trust the Lord when the sun is shining and it's seventy-two degrees, but when you're standing at the edge of the cliff, and the only way out is to jump, it's pretty hard to trust. Yet, we needed that refrigerator, and no donation was available, so on a Thursday, I ordered a new commercial refrigerator. They promised to deliver it on Tuesday.

On Monday morning, I went to work at my church, and a note was on my desk. A faithful Catholic friend, who attended Mass every morning, had stopped by my office on her way home from worship. Her note told me there was a gift for me in my desk drawer, and when I opened it, I found an envelope with $2,000 in cash. Astonishment is the only way I can describe my reaction, followed by immediate praise and thanksgiving, followed by shame that I couldn't trust more.

I called my friend to thank her for this great gift. I also wanted to know why she left that amount at this time. Her response was, "The Lord told me you needed it. What do you need it for?" The refrigerator was delivered the next day and the bill came to $2,034. Lazarus House had the $34, and due to my friend's gift, we now had $2,034. Don't you *ever* tell me that God does not care about our every need, because I can prove that he does. That refrigerator is still working away today keeping food safe for the hundreds of people Lazarus House feeds every week.

CHAPTER 8

A SECOND SEASON

Have you ever had a house blessing? It's a wonderful way to celebrate and invite God's presence into a new home, and we sure had a lot of celebrating to do in June of 1998. We gathered in our new home at the St. Charles Free Methodist Church, thanking God for our blessings and asking his continued guidance and protection as we moved forward to serve our brothers and sisters in his name.

The front door of Lazarus House

The main floor of emergency shelter

You may remember the lady who showed up at the community meeting at city hall in 1997 and told me she had already worked with the students at the high school to raise $1,000? Well she didn't stop there, and neither did her family. Her husband is a gifted carpenter, and he volunteered to build beds for us. I had been wrestling with the problem of how to fit everyone into the space we had been allocated, and one of our guests (my daughter's renewed grade school friend, "Bobby"), had suggested bunk beds. Brilliant! Except that I didn't have any money to buy them. Then Steve stepped forward, offering to not only design and construct the beds, but also get the materials donated, so the beds would not cost us anything. How could it get any better?

A staff person was now on board, and while he couldn't be there seven nights a week, he was there at least five, which meant that I only had to step in the other two nights. Of course we augmented him with other volunteers so there was always more than one person to help our guests, and we had a regular lineup of volunteer groups to provide meals daily. Every night some kind community group brought in a hot meal to serve all our guests, both the ones who stayed with us and those in the community who had housing but needed some help with food. The volunteer group also brought food for breakfast and bag lunches, so our guests had food to take away with them when they left in the morning.

Within five days of setting up shop at our new location, our numbers doubled. It was as if God had been holding back the floodgates, and now that we were "home," our guests flocked in. At this time, we were fortunate to be able to provide what we did, and having the shelter open during the daytime hours as well wasn't possible. It bothered me that we had to send our guests out every morning, but at least they had a home base and a safe place to store their belongings. They were able to come in every evening at five, and they knew they would be greeted by smiles, nourishing food, shower and laundry facilities, and a safe place to rest. We were doing amazingly well, especially considering how "young" we were. And yet, I still had a sense that there was so much more we could and should be doing.

The second week we were at our new "home," I was helping our guests get ready to leave for the day on a Sunday morning. As always, I encouraged everyone to worship at a church of their choice, but I knew that most of our guests would not. They didn't have a church home, and they felt uncomfortable walking into a church they didn't know, thinking that people would be pointing them out because they were homeless. Our guests didn't wear signs saying, "I am a homeless person," but when one is homeless, there is a tendency to feel "less than," and that's difficult to overcome.

God convicted me that we needed to provide a worship opportunity at Lazarus House on Sunday mornings. In my typical fashion, I became angry at God. I remember telling him, "It is never enough? Where am I supposed to find someone to conduct

Sunday worship? Can I never catch a break here?" In his typical fashion, he was politely silent, but his "suggestion" to find a way to offer Sunday worship was not withdrawn. So now what?

On Monday morning, I went to work at my church and got a phone call from someone I didn't know. He said he had been convicted that he was supposed to come to Lazarus House and offer worship on Sunday mornings! When was I going to learn to stop complaining and just trust God for solutions?

The following week, Mark showed up on Sunday morning, all set to offer a worship opportunity to our guests before they left for the day. Mark had a bit of a "John the Baptist" look about him, complete with long hair. I remember that the volunteer who was with me that morning looked a bit disconcerted at meeting Mark, and politely asked me when we were alone how well I knew Mark. I told the volunteer that I didn't know Mark at all, but I knew he would be perfect because God sent him. Mark volunteered at Lazarus House for many years, not only conducting Sunday worship but also offering a midweek Bible study. And as expected, over time it was clear that once again God had sent his best.

So we had a permanent home, a staff person, lots of volunteer support, and the determination that we would stay open year-round. I continued to work full time at my church and did my best to juggle my responsibilities. More and more it became difficult for me to get everything done properly. God isn't lazy, and he doesn't do slipshod work, and he doesn't expect us to, either. I was often up all night writing grants, and then tried my best to work all day with little or no sleep. I was not a young woman, and clearly I could not keep this pace up indefinitely.

The holiday season of 1998 was especially demanding for me. We had our now annual "Thanksgiving Feast" for our guests and the community, and it was a big hit, but took lots of time and energy. Right from there, we swung into the "giving" season, and lots of folks wanted to know what they could do to help our guests at Christmas. Couple that with my responsibilities at my church for the Advent/Christmas season and my responsibilities at home, and you had one very overworked lady. I knew something had to give.

I prayed about what to do, and it seemed the best option was to hire someone part time to handle some of the administrative details with which I was struggling. One of our faithful volunteers was between jobs, and I thought she would be a perfect fit, so I called and asked her to meet with me. In our meeting, I began to explain what the needs were, and in the middle of my explanation, God said, "You know, you're doing this backwards." Just like that, I knew he meant I was to leave my position at church and go work at Lazarus House full time. I was so grateful that I was talking to a faithful woman, because she understood entirely when I told her that God had just spoken to me. I had to stop the interview and go find my pastor immediately so I could tell him what had happened and let him know I had to submit my resignation.

No one of good conscience would leave a church staff during the holidays, so I stayed on through Christmas. But in January of 1999, I left my full-time position at my church and started showing up every day at Lazarus House. It was a great blessing to have more time to get things done properly at Lazarus House, but there was also the matter of a paycheck for me that would now be missing.

My husband has always been a wonderful provider for our family, and my children have never been demanding about their needs. Yet, we felt convicted to send them to Christian schools, and the tuition bills were not small. When I told my husband about God's direction to send me to Lazarus House full time, he said with his typical rock-solid faith, "God will provide." It's fine to say that, but we were now going to have to actually live that conviction, and that can be scary.

Newspapers were now a regular part of our Lazarus House culture, and while I was careful to protect our guests and not allow the newspapers to put them on display, I was grateful for the coverage we got, not mentioning names or showing faces, but letting the community know the need.

During the holidays, we had lots of visits from reporters, and during one of them, I happened to mention that I was going to be leaving my position at my church and coming on staff at Lazarus House full time in January. The reporter asked me how I was going to get paid, and I told them that I really didn't know, but that I was trusting God for provision. They did a sidebar in their Lazarus House holiday story about this, and at the beginning of January, I received a note from a business owner in the community I had never met.

He said he read the story in the newspaper about me leaving my position at church so I could be at Lazarus House full time without knowing how I would get paid. He said he didn't want me to worry about that, so he enclosed a check for $500 and told me I should expect one of those to arrive every month!

Again and again over the years, God has tapped people on the shoulder and told them that they were to provide for a specific need at Lazarus House. Whether it was a refrigerator, a building renovator, a Sunday worship leader, or a paycheck for a staff person, God kept sending just what we needed when we needed it. I was beginning to trust more and more, and I sure would need that for the journey ahead.

CHAPTER 9

TRUST IS A MUST

My husband and I bowled with our church league for many years. Well, they bowled; I showed up and threw the ball. Try as I might, my ball would seldom go where I thought I had aimed it, and my husband kept telling me that my basic problem is that I was trying to steer the ball. He said I should just go up to the line and throw the ball as I had been shown and let the ball do the rest of the work. I thought I was doing that, and yet the result was so poor that it was clear I was not. This problem persisted for me in many other areas of my life too.

By the spring of 2000, we were bursting at the seams. We had been as creative as we could be, and the bunk beds our guest had suggested and our faithful volunteer built were a great help, but we were out of space. It was especially hard for our women and children, who needed some semblance of privacy. Our host church had been extremely generous sharing their space with us, but they didn't have any more to share. What were we to do?

I was standing in the middle of Lazarus House one afternoon, looking out the windows that overlooked the courtyard of the U-shaped church building, and asking God earnestly for an answer to our problem. He immediately drew my eye to the east wing of the church, pointing out that this wing was a one-story wing, while the other two wings of the church were two stories.

He said, "Wouldn't it look nice if the east wing were a two-story wing too?" And that was all he said.

What a great idea! Except now I had my next big assignment: find out how possible it would be to add on to the church. I had many questions about this project. Was it structurally possible to add a second story onto this wing? Would the church allow us to do this? Who could we get to build this? Finally, how would we pay for this?

All journeys begin with the first step, so I asked around about reliable local architects and assembled a short list of names. I prayed about whom to contact first, and one name seemed to jump up off the list at me, so I gave him a call.

I had never met this man and had no idea if he knew anything about Lazarus House, but I did my best to explain to him what our need was, careful not to tell him outright that God had directed me to call him, lest he write me off as a lunatic. I ended my explanation with an invitation for him to come to Lazarus House to examine the property so he could get an idea of what it looked like and gauge how possible it might be to add a second story on the east wing.

This man told me that he didn't have to come over, and that he knew we could add a second story. I was astounded and asked him how he could be so sure about this. He told me that a few years ago, when the Congregational Church had owned the building, they were trying to make an informed decision about whether to add on to their property or relocate, and in order to make that decision, they had hired him to draw up plans for a building addition. The plans he drew up called for a second story on the east wing of the building. The Congregational Church decided to relocate and sold the property to the much smaller Free Methodist Church, who now had room to host Lazarus House at their site. The architect told me he thought it was odd, but for some reason he had saved those plans all these years, and they were still in his basement.

Jeremiah 29:11 says, "For I know the plans I have for you," declares the Lord, "plans to prosper you and not to harm you, plans to give you hope and a future" (NIV). I've read that scripture many times and never realized that God's plans can include actual blueprints, but in this case, they did!

So, we had the plans and the architect to help see the plans through to completion, but we had no money and no one to do the actual building. There was also the "small" matter of asking the church for permission to tear up and reconstruct their building. All these "minor" details are just that to God: minor details. One by one, he solved every problem.

Our host church was gracious as always when asked to extend themselves even further to accommodate Lazarus House's growing needs. Little did we all know how long this project would actually take and how much inconvenience they would be subjected to, but I sense that even if they had known, they still would have given us permission. God's people are dependable, generous, and obedient. They believed me when I told them this was God's idea and offered as proof the fact that the plans already existed. Awesome!

Once the idea was announced (and God bless the Lazarus House Board for yet again going along with another seemingly outlandish idea), the community started to come together to support it. Of course a building addition of this magnitude would not be cheap, but I had no idea how much it would actually end up costing.

Donations began to trickle in, and I was on the lookout for any grant opportunity out there. While we depended on God's provision, we knew that he sometimes provides through others, so we were not opposed to taking money from the government. Lazarus House was a ministry, and we were very clear about that. But we did not insist that anyone receiving care through Lazarus House first profess their faith in Christ, nor did we insist that anyone partake in worship or Bible study. This is the way Jesus gave it to me, and I think it is in keeping with his character. Jesus never asked if anyone believed before he healed them, but through the healing he provided, many came to believe. So it was with Lazarus House; all were welcome, and care was provided without questions about anyone's belief. As a result, many did come to believe (or confirm their belief), and we were able to qualify for government grants because we wouldn't refuse to serve anyone based on his or her belief or lack thereof.

Our friends at the county who controlled the CDBG funding had money available for capital projects, and our building addition certainly fit that criteria. We wrote a grant for some CDGB money, and they came through for us again.

A major corporation in our community, had a foundation that funded capital projects, and our application to them was approved too. Another nice chunk of money came our way.

An application was submitted to HUD, the Housing and Urban Development federal agency, and it too was approved. However, they had many stipulations and reporting requirements that were very complex, and our ability to meet all those requirements was going to pose a real challenge. Again, God used a very bad situation for good, and blessed us.

Our town was the worldwide headquarters for Arthur Andersen, which provided financial consulting and oversight for corporations all over the world. The company had a reputation for employing only the brightest and the best, and for working its people very hard. One of their faithful employees had been a friend of mine for many years, and she is one of the smartest people I ever met. She worked almost as hard for Arthur Andersen as I did for Lazarus House, and she is honest and ethical and has strong Christian values. When the Enron scandal came along in late 2001, Arthur Andersen, its auditor, was blamed. A hasty court decision in Texas in early 2002, later overturned by the US Supreme Court, prevented the company from doing business any longer in Texas. As a result, the company rapidly unraveled, with tens of thousands of people globally needing to find a new place to work. And so it came to pass that my friend was out of a job in the corporate world, and ready to work directly for the Lord at a much reduced rate. God's timing is always perfect.

Because we were using some HUD funding, we had to adhere to strict guidelines about getting bids for the construction work. God arranged for a very ethical construction company in our hometown to submit the low bid, and so we now had an excellent contracting company that was family owned and knew what Lazarus House was about. Time and again they went out of their way to make sure the job was done right at the lowest possible cost.

Everything was lining up perfectly, but we still needed some funding. We owned no property and didn't have much money in the bank, but God prompted a local banker to look on us with favor. I don't know if this could happen in today's day and age, but back then when we needed help, the banker listened to our proposal and lent Lazarus House $400,000 with no collateral. This man is now home in heaven, but his picture and his story are hanging on the wall of the addition at Lazarus House so everyone can know what God can accomplish through human beings.

We still needed about $100,000, but construction would take at least one year, and I was confident that God could raise that amount in the next twelve months. Except, at the last minute, HUD informed us that they needed to see all the money on the table before they would allow us to begin construction. I was devastated! We had come so far and everything seemed to be in place, and now at the last minute to learn that it was all going to come to a screeching halt. There was no way we could raise $100,000 by the end of the week, which was the deadline HUD gave us.

I went to our board with this horrible news and asked them to pray with me that God would make a way where there seemed to be no way. The next day I got a call from someone who heard of our plight, and he said that he would write us a check for $100,000 as an outright donation. I was stunned! I knew this person and had no idea that his family had those kinds of resources. Many people are financially blessed but not everyone has a heart willing to share those blessings with his people for his purposes. This family will always know that it was their gift that made the building addition possible.

Construction began on the addition, and I would like to tell you that it went smoothly, and we had few problems. If I told you that, I would not be telling you the truth. Just because something is God's idea doesn't mean that implementing the idea is going to be trouble-free. Think of what Nehemiah had to contend with when he built the wall around Jerusalem. If God's hand is on something, it will be blessed. Through struggles and hardship, the next step in the Lazarus House story came to fruition: the Center for Transitional Living (CTL).

The Center for Transitional Living was a two-year program that provided a step up from the emergency shelter for those who were able and willing to take it. Candidates had to have some form of income and pay 10 percent of it monthly to help cover expenses. This was done as a way to help folks get used to paying bills again. CTL residents had their own rooms and met with their case managers weekly, budgeting all their money and working on goals they set for themselves. If they successfully completed the program, they would receive 10 percent of the 10 percent they had paid. This money often helped pay their security deposit and first month's rent on an apartment.

Now that we were going to be able to offer this next step to our guests, we needed someone dedicated to this specific ministry. I had taken some of our guests to a monthly clothing giveaway one of the churches in our community sponsored. While waiting for our guests to select clothing, a woman came up to me and introduced herself. She said she knew of Lazarus House and would like to come and see it. She said she had quit her job just that week because God was directing her to do full-time ministry work. She didn't know what that work might be, but she left her full-time job on faith, believing that God would provide a next step.

I was amazed at her faith. She didn't appear to be financially well off (something that turned out to be quite true), yet she left a paying position at the Lord's direction and was simply waiting upon him to show her the next step. Her visit to Lazarus House that week was life changing for both of us, and she joined our staff and headed up our transitional living ministry.

We now had strong ministry partners in all aspects of Lazarus House, from operations, to administration, to transitional living, and God had sent each and every one of them. Over the years, I have often been asked how I was able to assemble such an outstanding staff, and my response was always the same (and always completely true), "I didn't do anything; God sent every one of them." For believers, it was a heartwarming statement, and for nonbelievers, it sent them away scratching their heads and wondering how something so excellent could be created under the direction of someone who was so obviously foolish. They were right, of course; I am a fool for Christ, and I pray that I always will be.

CTL hallway

CTL lounge

CHAPTER 10

SATAN WITH SKIN ON

Lazarus House was no longer a start-up ministry; we were established and growing. Because we had God's favor, the community supported us, and we had good relationships with our neighbors, local churches and government officials, the police and fire departments, local benevolent organizations, and the schools and libraries. Such favor is not common for homeless shelters, and it was just more evidence of God at work.

But there was one area that God was not at work in, and he laid the problem on our doorstep quite literally. One night, as we were getting ready to lock our doors, we had an unexpected visitor. Lazarus House is an emergency shelter, and so we were used to having unexpected visitors. Our doors locked at 10:30 p.m., and our guests knew they needed to be "home" by then. Special arrangements would be made for those who worked late or had a special event, and if someone came after the time we normally locked our doors, and they were in need of help, we certainly would admit them if they came in peace, and do all we could to help.

On that night, I made welcome a young man whom I had never met but had heard of on the street. I sensed in my spirit that this young man was very frightened, and so I did all I could to put him at ease. I sat with him on the stairs in the hallway of the emergency shelter. The lights had been turned off, as it was bedtime, so only low-level lighting lit up the area in which we sat. I tried to keep this young man talking and tried to get him to tell me what it was that was upsetting him. I sensed that something bad had happened to him that evening, and I wanted to help him in any way I could.

In the midst of our conversation, he suddenly stood up and said, "I have to go." I tried to convince him to stay just a while longer, but he ran down the stairs yelling over his shoulder that he would be back. As I watched him run out the door, the Lord said to me clear as day, "You're here for the heroin kids." I knew that heroin was a problem in our community, but I had no idea what an epidemic it had become. I was extremely surprised when God said that to me and didn't know exactly what to make of it. I did not see that young man for another year, but I did learn the next day what had upset him. Another young man from our community had died of a heroin overdose, the circumstances of which have never been clear, and I suspected our nighttime visitor had some knowledge of this death.

I had never met the young man who died, but his parents designated his memorial money to be directed to Lazarus House, and so I attended my first "heroin" funeral and met this young man's mother. She was heartbroken, but very gracious when I introduced myself to her, and so began the next chapter in the Lazarus House story: the struggle against Satan with skin on, also known as heroin.

I grew up on the southwest side of Chicago, so heroin was not a new drug to me. It was the scourge of a community that bordered my neighborhood, and I saw firsthand how destructive it was. Back then, the only method of administration for heroin was to shoot it, and convincing suburban kids to stick a needle in their arms was a hard sell. The heroin manufacturers/distributors knew this, and they came up with a brilliantly evil plan. Rather than cutting the heroin as much as they did so they could get more product out of the crop, they made it more potent. Now that may not seem like a good idea, but the end result of cutting the drug less and making it more potent was that it could be snorted or smoked for the desired effect rather than shot. Suburban kids who would never have shot heroin were now introduced to the "wonders" of heroin via a laced joint or inhaling it like cocaine. Viola! A whole new generation of heroin addicts was born. Once they got a taste of this "wonder" drug, they were hooked almost from the start, and their lives became centered on the constant pursuit of heroin. Everything in their lives also became a "yet."

"Yets" are known to folks in the recovery community. They are the things you haven't yet done, and swear you will never do. Your addiction uses "yets" to convince you that things are not really so bad, because you haven't yet _____, and here you get to fill in the blank. It usually starts with something like: haven't yet used every weekend, and from there it goes to telling you that they haven't yet used every day, and so on. Of course, in short order you end up with all your "yets" becoming everyday realities. Heroin takes your freedom, your will, your dignity, your family, your education, your self respect, your health, and, finally, your life. Kids who would never have considered sticking a needle in their arms (or eyelids or some other inconspicuous place) now gladly do so, knowing that they can get a "better" high if they shoot heroin.

The largest poppy fields in the world are in Afghanistan. Please understand that this is not a coincidence. Terrorists can't fly their planes into all of our buildings, so they have found another way to destroy our civilization, by destroying as many of our young people as they can with heroin.

After I attended my first heroin funeral, we began to get young people coming through our doors who needed a place to stay. They weren't able to stay at home any longer, and their plight became clear quickly; they were addicted to heroin. In the early days, I didn't know that no outpatient treatment would work for heroin. The sad truth is that almost no treatment of any kind is greatly effective against this addiction, but in order to have any hope of recovery, the addicted person needs to be removed from his or her using environment and placed in an environment with no heroin available, and with recovery being the complete focus 24/7. It was heartbreaking to see these kids, usually in the area of nineteen, in complete bondage to something so evil. They would make promises and, at the time, I think they probably meant to keep them. But their addiction would not allow them to keep their word to anything but their drug. They would do anything to get heroin: steal from family and friends, shoplift daily, and sell their most precious commodity: themselves. Nothing mattered to them except heroin.

In addition to destroying them, their families were in ruins too. What do you do when something this alien and evil invades your family? We are not prepared to deal with this monster. If a burglar breaks into your home, you call the police. If a terrorist moves into your neighborhood, you call Homeland Security. Who do you call when something as evil as heroin inhabits your adult child? Parents would threaten, beg, plead and punish their adult child, all to no avail. Those who had been good students and kind, caring kids turned into people who dropped out of school, stole from their family members, and cheated and lied about everything. One of the moms I came to know well told me how she knew when her heroin-addicted son was lying—his mouth was moving.

As these ravaged young people began to show up, their parents began to contact us too. It was clear that parents needed support, and so we began to meet weekly to speak about the unspeakable, to share our sorrows and courage, and to pray. Oh how we prayed! The bravest prayer was that God would save our young people, doing whatever it takes. If you or someone you know is struggling with a friend/loved one with an addiction, please get in touch with the local Al-Anon chapter. Help and hope is available.

At times, I would get a call from a sobbing parent late at night, lamenting that his/her young person had just been arrested. To this, I would respond, "Alleluia!" I'm sure many parents thought I was out of my mind or cruel, but I would explain that at least now they knew where their "child" was, that he or she was off the street, and we could pray that God would use the incarceration for good.

Yet, the legal system often isn't kind to those with addictions. It's hard to be understanding to someone who has been arrested more than ten times for shoplifting on a grand scale, but these kids didn't need punishment; they needed treatment.

I was not the only one who felt that way. The judge who was in charge of the court cases for the young man who was my first heroin fatality was devastated by this young man's death. The judge knew that this young man was addicted and needed care, but the way the court system was set up, the judge could do no more than make suggestions and recommendations and sentence the young man to jail time. Of course, the minute he got out of jail, he went right back to heroin. This was a terrible situation for the young man, his family, and our entire community.

After this young man's death, the judge, who was a very committed Christian, vowed that he would get an alternative treatment court started in our county for those who commit crimes due to their addictions, no matter what it took. Thus began drug court.

It was amazing to see how the drug court grew and the effect it had on those in its charge and on the community. The judge assembled a team of dedicated workers, who would go into crack houses and bars at 3:00 a.m. and pull those under the auspices of the drug court out. There was literally nowhere to run and hide, and the judge was mercifully merciless.

You had the opportunity to sign up for drug court if you were facing a felony charge, if the underlying cause of that charge was your addiction, if you were willing to initially plead guilty to the charge, and if you were willing to undergo two years of strict supervision, drug testing, and treatment. At the end of the two years, if you successfully completed the program, your record would be expunged.

Over time, I saw the heroin problem begin to dwindle, one treated addict at a time. Oh, lots of addicted people were relapsing still, but there were less this month than last, and that trend continued. Those who did relapse were immediately put in jail, where they awaited inpatient treatment. There weren't enough treatment beds, and there was not enough money to pay for all the beds that were needed, so some people waited in jail for weeks and months before a bed became available. Addicted people are not known for their patience (they want it *now*), and so waiting in jail rather than getting into treatment immediately was not what they had in mind. They began to lose focus and hope.

And then God said to me, "Since we can't get them into treatment quickly, wouldn't it be great if we brought treatment to them?" What a great idea! I never would have thought of that. Not only had God come up with this great idea; he had prepared me for this task by sending me back to school.

Shortly after God revealed to me that I was here for the heroin kids, he told me I needed to know more so I could better help them. I was working sixteen-hour days and was trying to squeeze in time to still have a life with my family; I had no time to go back to school. I explained this to God, but he was adamant: learn more so you can help more. Remembering how it did no good for wiser people like Abraham and Moses and Jonah to argue with God, I reluctantly agreed and enrolled in a local community college's addiction counseling program. Two years of classes were followed by a year's internship at treatment facilities. The whole time I juggled all this, God kept me awake and on my feet. God is in charge of everything, including time, and if you trust him and follow his guidance, he can even expand your time.

The knowledge that came from this training surpassed mere academics, as I was blessed to get to know many people in the recovery community whose experience and wisdom were greater than anything in books. I was equipped well to help those who were addicted and their families. I also received training that helped me better assist with mental health issues, and that became very important too.

When God told me that the answer to those impatient persons in jail awaiting treatment was to bring treatment to them, by God's grace, I was ready. I called the judge in charge of the drug court and told him what the Lord had laid on my heart. He was delighted to hear this news and set about immediately to get me clearance to visit the jail weekly and do treatment groups with the men and women in drug court who were awaiting a treatment bed.

Did I need to add something to my already overloaded schedule? Absolutely not! Are we to follow God's direction even when it doesn't make sense, seems impossible, or we're convinced we're not up to the task? Absolutely! God doesn't call the equipped; he equips the called. If he calls you to it, he'll get you through it.

My weekly visits to jail to do treatment groups turned into a wonderful blessing in my life. We are called to house the homeless, feed the hungry, and visit those in prison. Prison ministry is not just a gift to those who are incarcerated; it is a gift to those who are visiting. To this day, I continue to visit with those in jail regularly, not because I have to, but because it is something God wants us to do, and it blesses me. It also continues to break my heart to encounter so many people who desperately want to change their lives, but know that upon their release, they will have no choice but to return to their old environment, which will probably mean an eventual return to their old lives. If we are serious about reducing the crime rate, we need to get serious about offering supportive housing for folks coming out of jail who want to make changes in their lives.

CHAPTER 11

ARE YOU OUT OF YOUR MIND?

My substance abuse training and my work with those struggling with addiction taught me an important lesson; many people become addicted to a substance because they have untreated mental health issues. When your thinking is confused, when you have constant mood swings, or when you hear voices, you want it to stop. You don't know what to do to get it to stop, but you know you want to feel "normal." Drugs and alcohol can dull your senses, so you're not as acutely aware of your mental confusion, mood swings, or internal voices. Of course, your behavior doesn't improve; in fact, it probably becomes much worse, and now you've got a compounded problem that is terribly tangled.

If someone has the dual diagnosis of substance dependence and a mental health issue, the first step is to remove the substance and let the person's brain chemistry return to whatever is normal for him or her. Only when the effects of the drugs are removed can an accurate mental health diagnosis be made.

As I visited those who were in the throes of an addiction, I heard more and more stories about how their lives were before drugs took them over. The more I heard, the more I realized that in many cases, these folks had some serious untreated mental health problems long before drugs came on the scene.

Lazarus House is not a treatment facility, but we support

treatment and recovery. It's important for us to know what we're dealing with, and it's important to know when to get help and to sort out the truly urgent (call 911) from very real needs that must be addressed, and soon.

The drug court helped those who broke the law due to their addictions get the help they needed, but what about the person who broke the law because of his or her mental health issues? How could treatment be made available to them? Especially when people have untreated mental health conditions, their judgment may be greatly impaired, and so trying to convince them that they need counseling and medication is nearly impossible.

If they are in trouble with the law and are facing some jail time, they may be open to options they wouldn't consider before. Another judge spurred on by the success of the drug court decided that our county needed another treatment alternative court, and so the mental health court was created.

No court is a panacea, but appropriately caring for people who have problems that impair their ability to live at peace in our society is a gift to all of us. The mental health court, much like the drug court, assists people with mental health issues and their families to understand, address, and better cope with their situations while providing the community with an improved level of safety.

I became involved in the mental health court, much like my involvement with the drug court, serving on its advisory board and doing all I could to help the community understand the importance of these alternatives to punishment.

Yet, many of the people we encountered at Lazarus House with mental health or addiction issues hadn't been in trouble with the law. Their lives were in tatters, but they had a clean record and no court involvement. How were we to help them? We would encourage people to get care, and in some cases, make receiving that care a condition for staying at Lazarus House. But what about the person who is too mentally ill to understand his or her circumstances?

One such person came through our doors and into our lives, and taught me many valuable lessons. "Ray" had lost everything: his home, his car, and his family. Because he was over the age of sixty-five, he was receiving Social Security and was eligible for Medicare, but none of that had helped him very much. When he came to us, I was puzzled about where his monthly Social Security money was disappearing to. "Ray" had a successful career in past as a builder of custom homes, so his income was quite good, and therefore his monthly Social Security check was not tiny.

My puzzlement soon turned to dismay when I began to see the number of letters "Ray" was writing every day. He would comb newspapers and magazines, looking for offers of "free money" or "free automobiles" or "free vacations." He entered every "contest" and gladly sent in the "registration fee," knowing that this would be the time he would hit it big. Because he did have some income, he could buy stamps and envelopes and paper, and did he ever! No one could persuade him that this stuff was a scam, and he was throwing his money away.

"Ray" had an unusual hobby; he played Monopoly with people no one else could see. He would set up the board and distribute the recommended play money to each "person," and then he would take turns for everyone, all the while carrying on an animated conversation with his "friends" that only he could see. He would also have long one-way conversations with his children, who had long ago written him off and refused to speak to him. His explanation about all of this was that he was telepathic, and he was communicating with his children and his Monopoly friends by telepathy. This was his created reality, and he would hear of no other.

I was perplexed about how to help "Ray." As only God can arrange, I encountered an attorney in the community who had a heart for people with mental health issues. His wife was a psychiatric nurse, and so he well understood the problems these people were facing. He knew that they were often their own worst enemy, because their confused mind told them they were just fine, and they didn't need any help. He was wonderful in getting emergency guardianships in place in situations where someone's mental health was endangering his or her safety. I called one of "Ray's" relatives to see if she would be willing to consider filing for guardianship. She told me that no one in the family would do anything to help "Ray." It seems that "Ray's" penchant for scams went to an earlier habit he had of scamming others. He had scammed just about everyone in his family out of money, and everyone was done with him.

I gave up on the idea of family intervention and continued to pray for God's intervention. It came in the form of a late night phone call from a police officer in a town about seventy-five miles away. It seems that "Ray" had been discovered wandering around in an unsavory part of this town earlier in the evening. "Ray" apparently had been beaten and robbed by someone, and he was wandering in a dazed condition. He had the presence of mind to tell the police officer that he lived at Lazarus House, and so the officer called us. By God's grace I was working late, and so I was able to speak with the officer. He told me that a kind cab driver from their community was willing to drive "Ray" back to us for only $50, but "Ray" had no money, and the police didn't have any funding for this type of situation either. I told the officer to please send "Ray" home to us and that I would pay the cab driver. God bless that police officer and cab driver for trusting us to be good for our word and cover the cost.

Upon his return home, "Ray's" story was heartbreaking. It seems he had found an offer for a "free car" and had contacted the person in the ad. They asked "Ray" how much money he had, and he told them how much his Social Security check was. They asked him when he would receive it, and he was then instructed to cash it the day he received it and meet them at a certain place in their community. "Ray" cashed the check and got on the train for the downtown Chicago station, which was the only way he could catch a train to the meeting location. It took "Ray" hours on various trains, but he finally arrived and was treated to a beating and a robbery, but no free car. This could not go on.

I called his relative back and begged her to help. Under the circumstances, she agreed that something must be done, and she contacted the attorney and went forward with filing for guardianship. "Ray" was served with papers informing him that he had to appear in court for a hearing to determine his competence. He was sure the judge would understand that he wasn't mentally ill but rather telepathic, but just to bolster his case, he spent hours at the library copying articles and taking notes on telepathy. He went to court with a multitude of documents, and, much to my surprise, the judge remanded "Ray" to the local state mental hospital for an evaluation. In all my years, I had never been able to get anyone admitted to the state mental hospital. I thank God for intervening for Ray.

Once upon a time, many states had large mental institutions. Some were well run, and some were not. All were expensive to operate, and so when psychotropic drugs were first discovered, the prevailing thought was that there now was a magic bullet that would make all mentally ill people "normal," and there would be no need for mental institutions. Mental health treatment professionals with every good intention went around medicating most of the people in the institutions and discharging them, because they would now be fine. Except they weren't fine. There is no "one size fits all" psychotropic medication, and even if a person initially responds favorably to a certain medication, he or she needs to be monitored carefully, as his or her response to the medication may change drastically over time.

But no matter, we had solved the problem of mental illness and could now save millions of dollars by closing down many of our mental institutions. Much of the money that would be saved by closing these institutions would now be directed to community-based mental health clinics, where people could get care at a fraction of the cost of operating the institutions. Except much of that money never got directed to community-based mental health clinics, and many of the people that were medicated and sent on their way in hopes that the community clinic would care for them had nowhere to go. It's hard to keep yourself clean and organized when you're homeless, and so lots of people who are homeless give up on trying to take their medication because they can't afford it and can't even find it amid the detritus of their belongings. Not only did we not solve the problem of mental illness, we now compounded it by making many of those affected with mental health problems homeless.

"Ray" was to stay at the mental hospital for at least two weeks, during which time he would be thoroughly evaluated to determine his mental status. A primary piece of this evaluation was a physical exam to determine if there were any physical conditions that could be contributing to "Ray's" behavioral issues.

One of the things that "Ray" always told me was that he was "as strong as a horse. I'm just like I was when I was twenty." I would smile and had to admit that "Ray" appeared trim and fit. Of course, he may not have had regular access to food for some time before coming to stay at Lazarus House. Still, I was not aware of any health problems. I was completely amazed when I received a call telling me that "Ray" had advanced prostate cancer and was being transferred to a medical facility. He died about two weeks later.

I also learned that "Ray" was diagnosed with bipolar disorder. I would not have guessed that due to his delusional behavior. What was explained to me is that if someone has bipolar disorder, and they are not taking medication and therefore have frequent bouts of mania, the chemicals that are released by their brains during their manic episodes can, over time, cause actual organic brain damage. As time passes, that damage can become permanent and irreparable, and the person can have a psychotic break from which there is no return; hence, the Monopoly game and the telepathy. While this certainly does not happen to everyone with bipolar disorder, it happened to "Ray."

If someone is ill, why wouldn't they want to take medication to help them get well? Someone with bipolar disorder, especially if his or her disorder runs toward the manic side rather than the depressive, can be very opposed to medication. Wouldn't you like to get up every day after only two or three hours sleep, ready to take on the world? Wouldn't you like to feel as if you're the world's best singer, dancer, artist, parent, etc.? You're Superman, able to leap tall buildings in a single bound, run faster than a speeding train, and dodge bullets. Medication takes away those manic feelings and replaces them with a more normal state. Suddenly you need seven or eight hours of sleep, and you realize that you sing off-key and your parenting skills need a lot of help. No more Superman (or Wonder Woman) for you. However, if you stop taking those hated pills that caused you to put on weight anyway, Superman comes back.

One of the things "Ray" taught me (besides some really interesting Monopoly rules) was that people who are in the grips of a severe mental illness often are out of touch with themselves somatically. "Ray" really believed that he felt like he did when he was twenty and that he was as strong as a horse. His created reality prevented him from being in touch with his body well enough to detect any feelings of illness, so his cancer went undetected.

It is so hard to know what to do when your loved one is diagnosed with a mental health condition. A wonderful organization exists to help family and friends of those with mental health issues better understand and cope: NAMI (National Alliance for the Mentally Ill). If you or someone you know would benefit from NAMI, please find your local chapter and get in touch with them. There are too many family members of "Rays" in our world who are discouraged and brokenhearted. Thanks be to God, there is hope and help.

CHAPTER 12

WOMEN AND CHILDREN FIRST

I have never felt very good about the way women are often treated. Granted, things have improved over my lifetime, and yet I still encountered many women who had been brought up with little self-worth and did not want but rather desperately needed a man. And the man they picked was often the worst choice possible. They suffered, and their children suffered.

Lazarus House is an emergency shelter, and as such, we offer hospitality and care, but we do not provide treatment. Because we were not limited to providing care for a specific population, we have people with every conceivable disadvantage come through our doors. While we don't provide any treatment, we do connect with treatment providers in our community so that our guests can get care through them.

But while we don't provide treatment or counseling groups, we knew we needed to do a better job of providing care for our ladies and their children. They needed a place that was a real home. Lazarus House was warm and welcoming, but it had the feel of a shelter. Our women and children had separate sleeping quarters from our men, but everyone ate in the same dining room, which also doubled as a recreational space

One day as I was getting out of my car, I saw that our neighbors had put a "for sale" sign in their window. The Lord said, "Pay attention," and I began to pray about what he would have us do. One of our faithful staff came to me that same day and asked if I had seen the "for sale" sign. When you're wondering if something is from the Lord or if it's pickles and ice cream, you look for confirmation and ask the Lord to give it to you. If it is from him, he will be faithful to show you. When this faithful staff woman asked me if I had seen the sign and what I thought of it, I knew I had my confirmation.

I knocked on the neighbors' door and asked to see the property. They were very kind and took me on a tour, and I came back to Lazarus House feeling disappointed. The downstairs of the house was being used as an antique store, and the small rooms were jammed with antiques of every variety. The upstairs was a small two-bedroom apartment that couldn't possibly accommodate more than four or five people. This simply would not suit our purposes.

Yet, the Lord kept bringing it to mind, so a few days later I stood on the sidewalk in front of Lazarus House and across the street from this building. I asked God to make me smarter than I am and show me how to use this house. Immediately, a plan came to mind. Now if I have an idea, I have to roll it around for a while, refining details and looking at things from every angle. If the Lord gives me a plan, it comes to me all at once with many details filled in. This plan was definitely not born of my thought process, chiefly because I'm not creative enough to think this way.

The Lord said, "You're looking at this the wrong way. What if no one slept here, but you used the house as a day center for women and children. You could also use the second floor for office space, which you really need." And that's all he said. Brilliant plan! But now I had to go forward to figure out how to do all of this. Did I mention that we didn't have any money to purchase the building? Those things are just details to God.

I hadn't yet sprung the idea on our always faithful board and was planning to do that at our next monthly meeting. But before the meeting took place, I was contacted out of the blue by a foundation in Chicago. We didn't know anyone at this foundation, and they didn't appear to be overtly Christian. We welcome everyone and do not insist that anyone worship or profess Christianity in order to receive help, but we are very clear about the fact that we are a Christian ministry and this is our motivation for doing what we do. I found it hard to believe that a secular organization from Chicago that did not know us was offering to fund us to the tune of $100,000 for any capital project we had in mind, but that was exactly what they did. Strangers don't ever come to you and offer you large sums of money, unless you're Lazarus House. To me, this was more confirmation that this was the Lord's direction.

When I spoke to our board about the building, I was able to tell them that it appeared the Lord had already provided a down payment. They agreed (bless them) that this was a good plan, and we should move in that direction. Now, all I had to do was get clearance from our city's Zoning Commission.

The man in charge of the Zoning Commission was a very kind person, who wanted to help Lazarus House, but he had to be fair and ethical, and I would expect nothing less. We had no problem when we opened the emergency shelter in a church, because since apostolic times it's been the mission and ministry of Christian churches to house the homeless and feed the hungry. As long as the primary function of the building is a church, there should not be any zoning issues. However, we were now looking at a commercial building, and the game was changing.

We met in his office, and he took out his large book with all the zoning regulations. He told me that there were no codes that applied to homeless shelters, and if we were going to purchase and use this commercial building, we would have to get a special use permit. That would take quite some time and require public hearings. I could just imagine what might happen at a public hearing, and even if the result was favorable, the time it would take to go through the process would mean that we could not accept this grant, as there was a deadline by which the money must be used.

I was very disappointed and sat in this man's office telling God that it's not fair that he brought us this far just to let us down. I was also trying to be thankful for a clear answer, and the sincerity of my thankfulness was really in question, because I did not want to hear a no. In the middle of my prayer complaint, the Lord said, "Look down." The zoning official had placed a map on the desk in front of us, which had squares drawn on it representing the various properties in the neighborhood. The squares had addresses on them only and no indication of what the building housed. At first, I did not comply with the Lord's command because I was too busy whining, so he told me a second time, and this time, it was "*Look down*." When I glanced down at the map, the Lord drew my attention to a property across the street from the building we wanted to purchase.

That building was built in place of a teardown, and it was a very nice-looking building that housed some commercial space on the ground floor and some apartments on the second floor. I presumed the commercial space would be occupied by a lawyer or real estate agency, but instead the Lord put an outpost for the local community mental health and substance abuse counseling agencies there. I'll never forget the day I had gone to check on the progress of renovations at our soon to be permanent site, and I saw someone lettering the windows on the new building. I drove slowly by, expecting to see a sign indicating a business, and instead saw the name of the local mental health and substance abuse counseling agencies. I sat in my car with tears streaming down my face praising God for his goodness to us. And now this same building held the key to our women and children's day center.

In this building, they had space for counseling groups and offices. No one slept there, so it was not a shelter. We were going to use our new building for the same purpose: counseling groups and offices; no one was going to sleep there, so there was no problem.

I stopped the zoning official midsentence and told him we had been looking at this all wrong. While Lazarus House was a shelter, the purpose of this new (to us) house would be for counseling and offices. I pointed on the map to the nearby property that housed the mental health and substance abuse agencies, and explained that they used their building for the same purpose we were going to use our building. There are many buildings in the downtown area, and he wasn't aware of the specific use of the nearby building, but he knew I wasn't a liar (and I suspect he would be diligent to check out what I said so he would catch me if I did lie), and if what I said was correct, there were no problems. He snapped his large zoning regulations book shut and wished me a good day.

Genius! God tells us not to worry what we are going to say when we go before the judge, that the Holy Spirit will give us the words. He sure came through that day. He was faithful to continue to provide in wondrous ways for this building, which eventually included a beautiful sunroom and a playground in the backyard for our children.

Women's Center

Women's sunroom

We needed someone knowledgeable who could oversee the renovations of this building. A few years before, God sent a man to oversee the kitchen for our Thanksgiving Feast. This feast now hosted about three hundred people, so getting all the food organized and safely served was no small task. A man with shaggy long hair volunteered to supervise the kitchen, and he did a bang-up job. At the end of that afternoon, I asked him if he would consider doing it again next year, and he said he would like to. He then said he wanted to help in other ways too and handed me a check made out to Lazarus House for a very large sum. I almost fell over. He sure didn't look like he had resources that would allow such a generous donation, but God has taught me again and again to never judge by appearances. As it turned out, this man had built a very successful business in our town and now was looking for a way to add more meaning to his life. He could afford to take time away from his business, and so he began to give much of his time to us, overseeing the renovations. Once again, God sent us his best, and his timing was impeccable.

CHAPTER 13

THE NEXT THING

Must there always be a next thing? I asked God that very often during the early days of Lazarus House, but by now I not only was accustomed to a "next thing" but actually looked forward to it, wondering what it would be and when it would arrive.

My answer came one winter day when someone knocked on our door and asked us to partner with them in creating subsidized housing for our community. Now if you know anything about grants, you know how difficult they are to acquire. Many long months, perhaps even years are spent establishing the groundwork to get ready to submit a complicated grant application. Hardly ever does someone knock on your door and tell you that they would like to fund you. But then, of course, most grants don't have a supernatural power overseeing the process.

This agency had a special fund to subsidize affordable housing whose source was a tax levied on real estate transactions. That past year the affordable housing fund had been "swept," when some of the carryover funds from the previous year had not been spent. They were determined not to have that happen again, so they made a concerted effort to encourage new applications in an effort to spend every dime in the current year's coffers.

Why did that agency knock on our door? One of our board members was active in the national affordable housing market, and I suspect he was one of the reasons we were approached. But beyond that, I know that God orchestrated this next step.

It had been on my heart for some time that we needed a next step. People coming to our emergency shelter had nothing: no home, no resources, and no hope. We began by providing a home and basic resources and all the hope they would accept. Many of our guests progressed to the next level: our Center for Transitional Living.

In order to qualify for the CTL program, the guests had to cooperate with their case manager, be compliant working toward the goals they set for themselves, and have some form of income. In the transitional program, the guests met with their case manager at least biweekly, and they had to bring an accounting, complete with pay stubs and receipts, for all their money. Ten percent of their income was paid to Lazarus House as a way to help our guests get ready for the real world, where they would be responsible for all the costs of daily living. The program could continue for up to two years, and if a guest successfully completed the program, 10 percent of the 10 percent he or she had paid during the time in CTL would be returned to him or her. This money was often used to pay the security deposit and first month's rent on an apartment.

Therein was the rub: finding housing that was affordable was very difficult. Many of our guests had deficits that would be lifelong. Their very best efforts would result in a part-time job at a fast-food restaurant at best. Or perhaps their deficit was such that they could not work at all, and had to live on Social Security disability, which is about $800 monthly. How can anyone live on that little income? The long-term prospect for these folks was rather dismal, and then came that knock on the door.

We now had a real chance to put some subsidized housing in place. The idea was not to build any housing but rather to partner with landlords in our community. The tenant would rent from the landlord, but the landlord would understand that Lazarus House would pay two-thirds of the rent on behalf of the tenant.

The tenant's name would be on the lease, and he or she would be expected to pay the remaining one-third of the rent on time. We would assure that would happen, as our case manager would meet at least monthly with the tenant and hold him or her to an agreed-upon budget. If the tenant had his or her one-third of the rent and sufficient money to pay the utilities, then Lazarus House would cut a check to the landlord for the other two-thirds of the rent. Landlords liked the idea because they knew we were dependable and would hold the tenant accountable. The tenants liked the idea because they knew they were getting help they absolutely needed to stay housed. And Lazarus House liked the idea because we knew it was the only way many folks could live with independent dignity. I suspect God was rather happy with the arrangement too.

We had a top-notch grant writer and a good administrative team, but we were going to need someone to head up our new housing program. I knew we better get some really qualified person, and then God brought Liz to mind. Liz was raised in our town. She had a degree in human services and worked in social services for two different not-for-profits that served our area. I knew her personally and knew of her work, and she was *aces*—Christ centered, kind, caring, smart, and compassionate, but tough when she had to be.

Up to now I hadn't recruited any of our staff; they all just showed up. When the executive directors of other not-for-profits asked me how I had assembled such an outstanding "cast of characters," I always told them very truthfully that I hadn't done anything; God had sent each one. Many received that news with skepticism or the belief that I was out of touch with reality. The truth is I'm *in* touch with a reality many folks don't understand.

This time, God was telling me to go and get someone, so I did. Liz's family was having a fiftieth birthday party for her at a local restaurant, and somewhere along the line it was mentioned to me that I should stop by if I had a minute. I brought Liz a small gift wrapped in birthday paper, and a very large gift sent via me but crafted by the Lord: an invitation to join the Lazarus House staff.

Liz was very surprised at my suggestion that she join the Lazarus House staff but did agree to come in to see me and talk about the idea in detail. When Liz came in, my explanation of her duties left her feeling overwhelmed and inadequate. She sent a nice note saying, "thanks but no thanks," and I called her to tell her that it was God's idea she come to work at Lazarus House. While it may be true that she didn't have all the gifts she needed, it didn't matter, because God had them, and he was not stingy about sharing. Liz humbly agreed to trust God, and so she turned in her notice and joined our staff.

For some time, I had been advised to put a succession plan in place. My response to the well-meaning folks who would tactfully raise this issue was that God would take care of it in his time. When Liz joined our ministry team, initially as a case manager for our women and then to head our housing subsidy program, I didn't realize at first that this was the succession plan God had in mind. But it was, and I am eternally grateful.

But having this new burgeoning program with the expanded staff it required presented challenges. Once again we were out of space, and once again God stepped up and arranged to have a house go on the market across the street from our emergency shelter.

The house had been occupied by a business called Bicycle Heaven. Now if that isn't a clear indication that God is in this, I don't know what is. Except that we didn't have any money; as if that has ever been a problem for God! It is said that God has all the money in the world; it's just in different people's pockets.

I stood outside this building one afternoon and said to God, "If you want us to have this building, you'll have to give it to us." And with that, I went on vacation. While I was away visiting my daughter in Florida, Liz called to tell me that a kind person from the community had called out of the blue that day and said he had been led to buy a house for us. He wanted to know if we had anything in mind. You just can't make this stuff up. God is never too small; I just sometimes underestimate him.

The house was rather compact, but we didn't need huge amounts of space. It was built in 1840 when Polk was president, but we had a board president who was nicknamed "MacGyver" (remember the guy with long hair who had showed up at the Thanksgiving Feast? Yep! He was now our board president), and was willing to give this project a lot of oversight time. I suspect he donated more than a few dollars as well.

Community Resource Center

Once the renovations were complete, we had a building that housed our outreach programs. Anyone who came to meet with our staff was greeted warmly and offered some of the nonperishable food we kept just for that purpose. Whether he or she was able to qualify for one of our subsidy grants (there are very strict rules around these grants that must be complied with), no one left without getting lots of information about where he or she could get help in the community for many other issues such as health care, utility assistance, and food pantries. If God can use things that are 150-plus years old to serve his purposes, he certainly can use you and me.

CHAPTER 14

HOLDING HANDS

Over the years I've learned the value of establishing and nurturing partnerships and alliances. It's important to do everything God is asking you to do, but it's also important not to do things he isn't asking or equipping you to do. I was always careful not to step outside the boundaries of our God-appointed mission, but it would break my heart to see needs go unmet. I would plead with God for solutions, and he was wonderful about providing resources. He also prompted me to keep attending all types of community meetings, where I would meet other social services providers. Every time I started to think that I was too busy to attend a meeting of some sort, God would admonish me that it was important, and I needed to make time.

The community mental health and outpatient substance abuse agencies moved into a brand new building across the street from Lazarus House the very month we opened at the Free Methodist Church. Only God could have arranged that. But while they were close by and their services were as reasonable as could be found, they had to meet their expenses, so they were not free.

And of course the situation with health care continued to break my heart. At the time, low-income persons were not able to receive Medicaid unless they had dependent children or were receiving Social Security disability. Many low-income single people had no health care and no hope of acquiring any. One of the best (or should I say worst) lessons I learned about this was when "Jim" broke his arm.

"Jim" had an accident and feared his arm was broken. He went to a hospital, and they examined him and took an x-ray, as is their legal charge. They told him that his arm was broken and that it was a simple fracture. They fitted him with an air splint and gave him a referral to a local orthopedic practice, telling him he should call them in the morning for an appointment. This is standard operating procedure for hospitals.

I stayed overnight at the Shelter that night, and "Jim" came in telling me of his plight. I gave him some ibuprofen and told him to be sure and call the doctor in the morning. "Jim" called and came to me to report that they refused to see him because he had no money or insurance. I told him I would take care of it. I was sure if I called, someone would be kind enough to see "Jim."

I called every orthopedic practice within a ten-mile radius of our town and no one would help "Jim." This man had a certified broken arm, and no one would agree to set it. I was incredulous and asked God for wisdom.

He reminded me of a kind man who went to our church. He was a family practice doctor, but I called him anyway and asked if he knew of someone who could help "Jim." He hesitated for a moment and then said, "Bring him to my office. I don't normally do this type of thing, but if it's a simple break I can set it, and it should heal fine." And that's just what we did. The arm did heal fine, and I will be forever indebted to this doctor for his kindness. But the problem still remained. How could we get care for all the "Jims" that would need help in the coming years? Somebody had to do something.

One fine spring day there was a knock on the door. The problem of health care was too big for me to solve but not too big for God. When I answered the door, I was greeted by a small group of folks who explained that they were connected to a free medical clinic in a town about ten miles north of us. Their board had decided that they were going to change from being a free clinic to a clinic that served Medicare and Medicaid patients. This group didn't feel comfortable with that decision so they wanted to strike out on their own and open a free clinic elsewhere. Did I think our town would be a good place for a free medical clinic? Are you kidding! I literally grabbed someone in the group and dragged them up the stairs to my office (which was roughly the size of a closet). We all squeezed in and spent the afternoon talking about possibilities.

After some conversation, we set out on a walkabout in our immediate neighborhood, with me pointing out some properties that might be promising. When we got to one vacant house located down the street from Lazarus House, the Lord spoke to one of the people in this group, and they made the decision to pursue purchasing the house and renovating it for use as a clinic. When I asked him about funding, he sheepishly told me that he planned to take care of that personally. When God sets out to do something, it will be spectacular!

The free clinic set up shop across the street from Lazarus House, and our local hospital partnered with them to provide care for many uninsured people in our community, including guests at Lazarus House. I will be forever grateful to them for all they have done and continue to do to improve the quality of life in our community.

Another spectacular thing God did was send us help with applying for Social Security disability. It's no small task, and most people had no idea how to go about it. Then too, almost everyone is turned down the first time they apply, and they give up and go away. In one of the many community meetings I attended, I met a man who was an attorney. His firm specialized in helping people apply for Social Security disability, and he offered to do an in-service training for our staff so we would be better equipped to help potential disability applicants wend their way through the system. He encouraged us to help seemingly qualified candidates apply without legal assistance initially. If they were successful, all was well. If they were turned down however, his firm would take a case if they felt it had merit. If someone was not approved, the law firm received no compensation.

If someone was approved, the law firm took a reasonable percentage of the initial back payment check the person received, and that was all. Of course, without legal assistance, the chances of someone's appeal being successful is almost nil, so getting the major portion of this back paycheck is much more than he or she would have received. Going forward, all the money received belongs to the deserving applicant for as long as the disability persists. Social Security disability is key for those who are truly unable to work, especially because it opens the door for medical care.

So now we had medical care in place, legal help with Social Security disability claims, and services for mental health and substance abuse close by. I was also able to make arrangements with some local inpatient substance abuse agencies, and our guests could be admitted for a reasonable fee. We wrote some grants to help cover expenses for treatment at these agencies, but it was never enough money to take care of all the needs. And needs certainly did exist.

"Barbara" was a very smart woman with a great sense of humor. She had wonderful family support and had held responsible jobs. She was also a serious alcoholic. She would live sober for a time and then have a relapse, and when she relapsed, she lost everything: her job, her home, and her self-respect. It was during one of these relapses that she came to stay at Lazarus House.

She was receiving outpatient treatment and going to AA meetings. She was beginning to look for a job again (she was an accountant) and thought she was on her way to rebuilding her life. No one knows what happened to cause her to relapse, but one night she didn't come home after her AA meeting, and I knew that meant trouble. "Barbara" rang the doorbell, and when I answered it, she could barely stand. Normally we don't allow people who are chemically altered to come into Lazarus House. We offer them the opportunity to get care via an ambulance, but they usually reject that idea and instead decide to leave for the night. That is a decision that concerns us greatly, but if we allow people to come in who are chemically altered, it can threaten the safety and sobriety of other guests who are struggling with their own issues.

This night, as I spoke to "Barbara," God spoke to me. "Let her come in," he said. Really? What about our other guests? I could smell alcohol on "Barbara" clearly, and if one of our guests who were working on their recovery smelled that too, it could cause them great distress. Still, the Lord was very clear, and I've learned that his ways are higher than mine, so I let "Barbara" in and helped her get to bed.

After she was settled in, I decided to spend the night too, so I could check on her frequently and make sure she was okay. But just as I was turning to leave the women's sleeping area, God spoke again. This time he said, "She isn't safe. She has something with her; you have to find it."

Oh, great, now I had to be a detective and search her personal belongings. I sure didn't want to do this, but God was very adamant, so I began to go through her belongings, looking for something that might harm her. Despite my best efforts, I could find nothing. I was turning to leave the women's sleeping area again when God said for the second time, "She isn't safe. You have to find 'it.'"

We are always careful to respect our guests, and one of the ways we do that is to allow them physical space. We never lay hands on our guests, and so for me to now lay hands on a sleeping woman was not something I thought appropriate. Yet I had done everything I could to find the problem, and all that was left was to see if she had anything on her person. I carefully rolled "Barbara" over and found that she was lying on top of a half gallon of vodka, and the bottle was full! She was able to conceal it in her winter coat, which she had refused to remove. I took the bottle away and dumped it. Had I not found it, she would probably have awoken in the middle of the night and drank a large portion of it. Given how intoxicated she already was, she might have died from alcohol poisoning. God had literally saved "Barbara."

In the morning, I told "Barbara" what had happened. She had no memory of the night before but believed me when I told her what had transpired. She called her brother, and the decision was made that she needed to go into inpatient treatment. She had been reluctant to do this until this relapse.

"Barbara" lived sober for several years but had a serious relapse again, and this time there was no one living with her to help. She died of alcohol poisoning, and the world lost a kind, generous, giving soul.

"Melanie" came to us after being asked to leave her home due to her drinking. Her live-in boyfriend had enough and gave her a choice of sobriety or the door. She chose the door.

We explained to "Melanie" that we supported sobriety and expected her to get help and stay sober. She said she would but didn't seem especially committed to the concept, until she found out she was pregnant.

This added a whole new dimension to the issue. "Melanie" didn't have a job or family support, and her boyfriend was done with her, so she had no idea how she could raise a child. It seemed to her that the best option was an abortion, something we begged her to reconsider. We told her we certainly understood if she didn't feel that she could raise the baby, but we would be happy to put her in touch with a responsible adoption agency that would find a loving home for her baby.

By God's grace (and many hours of prayer on the part of our staff), "Melanie" decided to keep the baby. Her pregnancy gave her the resolve to commit to sobriety, and "Melanie" worked a serious program. She got a job and moved into an apartment. We lost touch with her but prayed for her often and trusted her care to God.

About three years later, I got a wonderful letter from "Melanie," which included the program from her college graduation. It seems that she went back to school and got a degree in education. She was writing to tell us that she had a teaching job lined up in the fall, and she and her three-year-old daughter, who was the light of her life, were happy and doing very well. She thanked us for being there at her most difficult time, and credited God and Lazarus House for the life she now had.

I would love to tell you that this was the end of the story, but "Melanie" did not live happily ever after. We heard about two years later that she too had died of alcohol poisoning after a serious relapse. Addiction is no respecter of gender, intelligence, or economic status. We had to find a way to do more to help those who were struggling with addiction.

This time it was a phone call that helped with the problem. Earlier, I had spoken to the executive director of a local substance abuse treatment agency, asking him to consider writing a collaborative grant with us and the local community mental health agency, to a federal agency that funds mental health and substance abuse treatment. They had some set-aside funding for homeless services, and I thought this would be a good fit for all of us.

He took a look at the grant application and told me he thought it was too involved. Their staff couldn't handle the application process or meet all the compliance requirements should the grant be awarded. It isn't that they wouldn't be in compliance; it was just that the reporting requirements would be so onerous they would have to hire additional administrative staff just to keep up. I told him I understood and kept praying that God would find a way.

However, now, during this phone call, he explained that he had been thinking this over, and decided that maybe we should apply for this grant. Not only that, but he was offering his grant writer as lead on the project. Like I said, God does spectacular work.

Only we weren't awarded the grant. There were a number of reasons why, none of which made much sense to me, but I was not in charge of the decision, and there was no appeal process. I was very disappointed but trusted God to make another way and kept praying. It's important to PUSH: pray until something happens. Something happened the following year.

Again, I received a phone call from this same executive director, this time telling me that he wanted to apply for this grant again. I was stunned. After all he and his staff went through, and his initial reluctance, I was sure when we got turned down that would be the end of it. But he said he wanted to give it another go, expecting that they could use much of what was already in place from the previous grant. Their plan was to update and tweak the application to suit what we now better understood the federal agency wanted.

And so the second attempt was made, and it was successful. Not only that, but the grant covered not just us but the homeless shelter that served the north end of our county as well. The funding was very generous and allowed us to get mental health and substance abuse services for any of our guests who were in need of such care. Doesn't God do great work?

CHAPTER 15

OUTSIDE THE BOX

Lazarus House was cooking on all the burners. We had an emergency shelter that was open twenty-four hours a day, 365 days a year. We had a Center for Transitional Living that offered our guests a supportive next step on their journey back to independent living. Our women and children had separate quarters that were homey and inviting. We had subsidy programs in place for our guests who were ready to go back to independent living but were still in need of some support, with an outreach center so they had a comfortable place to come and meet with our staff. And underneath all of this, we had a caring staff of thirty-eight dedicated servants who did whatever it took to get it done. God had been so good to us!

We also had amazing support in the community. Let me tell you just one of the stories of this support. One spring day, I was contacted by a nine-year-old girl who said she wanted to sell some of her toys to help support Lazarus House. It seems that she had recently visited Lazarus House with her parents and some other people from her church. They were painting one of the rooms in the shelter when there was a tornado warning, and everyone had to be herded into the basement for safety. We stayed there for about an hour until the all-clear was sounded. During that time, all our guests, staff, and volunteers were crowded into a small space, but rather than complaining, we all made the best of it, making up games and singing songs. Ellen was especially taken with the children who were guests at the shelter, realizing they were just like her.

When she got home, she decided she needed to do more to help. She looked around her room and thought about all the toys she had. She asked her mother if it was ok for her to have a garage sale and sell some of her toys to raise money for the children at Lazarus House. Her wonderful mother told her she thought it was a great idea, and so Ellen's Excellent Sale was born.

Ellen did sell some of her toys that year, and her parents went through the house and found a few things they could put in the garage sale as well. We were most grateful for their donation but even more grateful to know there were people like that in our community.

The following year, Ellen decided that she could expand her efforts, and so she extended an invitation to her neighbors and church to participate in her Excellent Sale. The donations poured in, and Ellen had a two-day event that raised a considerable amount of money. Ellen also had volunteers from her neighborhood and church help at the sale, so it truly was a group effort.

Ellen continued to hold this annual sale until she graduated from high school. The event got to be so large that the mayor ordered the streets around Ellen's house closed during the sale. Ellen received recognition from the American Girl Doll Company, and she was featured in their magazine as an example of what American girls can accomplish. They held an "Ellen Day" at their store in downtown Chicago, and Ellen and some of her friends and family and I were treated to a very special day. Ellen visited with all the girls that came to the store that day, signing autographs and encouraging the girls to find a way they could serve their community too. The American Girl Doll Company gave both Lazarus House and Ellen's school a check for $5,000, and staff from the company came down from their headquarters in Wisconsin and attended Ellen's Excellent Sale that summer.

Ellen's Excellent Sale

This past May, Ellen graduated from Moody College in Chicago. She was looking for an employment opportunity in ministry, and she was offered a position as the special events and volunteer coordinator at Lazarus House. She accepted the position and now will be serving God full time through Lazarus House. Thanks be to God!

Another way our community support was evident was in our relationships with our city administration. From the mayor's office to the police chief to the code enforcement officer, they all knew we were here to help, and we knew we could rely on them as well.

Our mayor surprised us one summer day during one of our

town's festivals by declaring the day "Lazarus House Day." We were awarded a plaque, and he read a proclamation stating that we were being recognized for all the good things we did in the community. That plaque is up at Lazarus House still as a testament to what God can do. I remember well going to the city council for the first time to address the proposed vagrancy ordinance, and now to see how this has all come full circle is beyond anything I could have imagined.

Our chamber of commerce too has given us several awards, citing our excellence in providing services and upgrading and maintaining the property we've occupied. Local service clubs such as the Rotary, Kiwanis, Lions and Exchange clubs have given us recognition and awards as well. There is no possible explanation for this except God's favor, and I will continue to thank him daily for all he has done and continues to do.

One of the surprising ways God used Lazarus House to help was through the code enforcement officer. Nobody likes to receive a notice that tells them they have to repair their gutters or paint their garage, but any well-maintained community understands that it's important for everyone's sake to uphold certain standards. Especially when there are issues concerning safety, the code enforcement officer's job is an important one.

So when the really nice code enforcement officer called to ask us for help, I was surprised, but ready and willing to do what it took. And so, another chapter in the Lazarus story was written. From people who were living in substandard conditions due to their inability to afford repairs, to people who were living in houses that were beyond repair, God had a part for Lazarus House to play.

I had some experience with folks who couldn't maintain their properties. Some years before, I had a man come to our door after he lost his property. He carried with him a letter from a real estate developer in our community, and the letter told the man how sorry the developer was that the man had lost his property. The letter suggested the man come to Lazarus House, and now here he was, standing on our doorstep.

This man had been a child in Germany in World War II. His father was conscripted into the German army and was never seen again. He lived in Dresden and was hiding in his neighbor's basement with his mother and younger brother while Dresden was being bombed. A bomb went into the furnace and exploded it out, wounding everyone with shrapnel. This man was wounded but was the only one who survived. At the age of twelve, he was left to wander the bombed-out German countryside, eating tree bark.

After the war, he made his way to America, where he enlisted in our military. He was extremely smart and did well at anything he attempted. He settled in our community and started a company that made specialty awards and trophies. I learned that he designed the first Super Bowl ring. He prospered and bought several properties around the community. But he had a problem; he had trouble throwing anything away. When you consider all the losses he endured as a child: his family, his home, his country, it's no wonder he wanted to hold onto anything he possessed. But at some point, all this "holding onto" becomes a stumbling block to your freedom and sanity.

His wife left him when she could no longer open the front door to their very nice home due to all the stuff he had stored inside the house. And then his son, who worked for NASA, was killed in an accident. I am told that after his son's death, he snapped, and no one could reason with him.

One by one, his properties were taken away. He would accumulate tons of junk on each property. The county would send him notices and levy fines, which he ignored. He was jailed more than once, but this too accomplished nothing. The county cleaned up his property at their expense, hauling literally tons of junk away in dump trucks. The next day, he would just start accumulating more junk again. Eventually, he lost all of his properties and ended up, a man in his seventies, homeless and friendless.

He stayed with us for about two years. One of his obsessions was bicycles, and he rode his everywhere, dragging a homemade cart behind so he could collect his junk as he went down the street. He would see a "treasure" and stop in the middle of the street to retrieve it. No one could dissuade him from this behavior. I had more than one call from the police telling me that they had found him late at night riding his bicycle on a dark road.

That behavior eventually killed him. He was riding his bicycle on a very busy street on a foggy night. A drunk driver didn't see him and hit him. He was thrown off his bicycle and landed in a farmer's field. No one knows how long he lay there, as the driver did not stop, and no one noticed the smashed bicycle on the side of the road due to the fog and darkness. I think of him often, and it always makes me sad. We tried to love him and give him a home. No one should end their days like that.

So when we encountered people who needed help to restore their housing, or needed a place to stay because their housing was beyond redemption, we were only too happy to help. We invited people to come to Lazarus House for a meal. We had amazing food—the best recipes lovingly prepared by people in our community and food from restaurants such as Red Lobster and from local grocery stores—but even more they enjoyed the camaraderie, visiting with our guests and finding friendship and fellowship.

At times we helped people restore their property. Our staff was already stretched thin, so how could we even begin to approach this problem? Where to start? There's a universal answer to that question: on your knees in prayer. We didn't have any funding to address these issues, and the property owners sure didn't either. Much of what needed to be done would require expertise that none of the staff possessed. But nothing is too hard for God.

We put the word out through our network of volunteers, and the phone started to ring. A church was willing to assemble a group and come for a Saturday. A men's group that included some people with carpentry, electrical, and plumbing skills lined up to help. Some people from our city's staff wanted to help too, and so a cadre of volunteers assembled.

One of the best gifts I ever received at Lazarus House was a humble woman of God named Carol who came to us as our operations manager. She adeptly juggled our operations staff, considering each person's need along with the need to staff our Shelter 24/7, 365 days a year. There are no holidays when you're doing homeless ministry. In fact, holidays usually bring more work for staff, as there are special events connected with many of them. Then too, our guests often had an especially hard time during the holidays, missing their homes and families and wishing they could have it all restored. Our staff would spend extra time listening to our guests and helping them feel cared for, especially during these times.

Carol never complained about having to rescramble the staff's work schedule yet again when someone turned up sick at the last moment. More often than not, she was the person to step into the breech when an unexpected hole opened up in the schedule. She was always ready to do whatever it took. Now what she volunteered to do was lead a cleaning crew for a house that was being restored. We all worked tirelessly to paint, scrub, rewire, replumb, and reinforce walls, windows, and anything else that needed repair. When the owners returned to their homes, they found property that was neat, orderly, and in full use. Thanks be to God!

Not only was the property restored, the property owners now had a friendship circle and knew that people cared about them. They knew where they could turn if they needed help, and they were able to help others by sharing their considerable skills and time with our guests.

In some cases, the house could not be restored, and the property owner had nowhere to live. They became welcome guests at Lazarus House, and we were able to work with them to help them overcome their circumstances. God uses Lazarus House in so many ways, and he's not done yet!

CHAPTER 16

A PORT IN THE STORM

God had used Lazarus House for so much more than I had ever imagined, and he had used so many of my experiences to help the ministry of Lazarus House be even more effective. However, I never saw this one coming; no one did.

August 29, 2005, was just another summer day to those of us who lived in the north, but to people who lived in the vicinity of New Orleans, it was a day that was to change their landscape and their lives forever. Like many of you, I watched the news of Hurricane Katrina making landfall, and I was grateful that it didn't do even more horrific damage. I remember going to bed thanking God that folks had been spared the worst.

In the morning, I awoke to the news that the levees had broken, and New Orleans was under water. I watched stunned and horrified as people were shown frantically waving from their rooftops, begging to be rescued, and no help came.

All day, the news was on at Lazarus House, and we all crowded into the dining room to watch. Our guests and staff alike were teary eyed and disbelieving. How could this be happening in America? On the whole, our guests have always had an attitude of gratitude, and never more so than this day when we all saw how many people had lost everything and were homeless and hopeless. What could we do? And then, the Lord reminded me of something

Sam and I did many times over when we worked with youth at our church: hold a car wash.

I asked our guests if they would like to have a car wash as a fund-raiser for the Katrina victims, and they were very enthusiastic. I telephoned a locally owned service station that was located on a corner of a major intersection in our town, and asked if they would be willing to allow us to have a car wash there as a fund-raiser for Katrina. They too were very enthusiastic.

That Saturday, with very little fanfare and just a couple of hand-lettered signs on poster board for advertising, a group of guests and staff set out with buckets and sponges, determined to wash as many cars as we could. We didn't set a price for the car wash, but made it clear that this was Lazarus House doing a fund-raiser for Katrina victims. None of us were prepared for what happened.

Cars began to stop and line up. Some people didn't have time to stop to get their car washed, so they literally threw money at us out of their car window. One person threw a $50 bill. An owner of a local restaurant drove by and saw what was going on. Around noon, he showed up with a very generous catered lunch so that none of our guests would be hungry. Hour after hour the cars lined up. Everyone told us what a great idea this was (of course it was a great idea; it was God's idea), and how touched they were that homeless people were concerned about helping the newly homeless Katrina victims.

At the end of the day, we were really tired but exhilarated that we had been able to raise over $1,000. Don't ever let anyone tell you that homeless people are lazy and don't want to work. That day will always live in my memory as one of my best.

But God wasn't through allowing us to help with the Katrina problem. Throughout the week, as we saw the horrors to which the people at the convention center were subjected, I continued to pray (I bet you did too), and then the phone rang. It was a friend who worked at the local Salvation Army. He had been recruited to go down to the registration center in downtown Chicago and help register people who were coming up from the New Orleans area via bus. Did I want to go and help too? I couldn't wait to get there. On the way down, Steve and I prayed together that God would send us exactly who he would have us help. I wasn't sure how this would all work, but I trusted God and knew this was of him. Steve and I spent the day greeting tired, anxious people, and any time someone would say that they had no idea where they were going to go, I asked them if they would like to come to Lazarus House. At the end of the day, we had eight families who needed help.

One family needed help that very day. They had been staying in a hotel on the south side of Chicago courtesy of a donation from a church. However, the church was out of money, and so this mom and teen daughter had to leave the hotel immediately. Steve and I made a plan to meet them later in the afternoon.

We drove to the neighborhood where the hotel was located. Traffic was at a complete standstill due to some police action, so Steve let me out, and I walked a couple of blocks to the hotel. When I arrived, I found that many of the hotel windows were broken, and yellow crime scene tape was draped across half the front of the hotel. The mom was waving at me from a room on the second floor, and she and I hauled suitcases, grateful that Steve was finally able to park on the street in front of the hotel. I couldn't get them out of there fast enough, and as we drove away, I thanked God for keeping us all safe.

In the 1970s, Sam and I led a group of volunteers from our church in resettling Vietnamese refugees. It was a wonderful experience and one that taught me many valuable life lessons. The difference between Katrina refugees and Vietnamese refugees was almost nil. They were homeless, unemployed, and had no possessions apart from a few clothes. There were also major cultural differences.

Drawing on my experience resettling Vietnamese refugees, I contacted the churches that supported Lazarus House (there were twenty-seven of them) and announced that we hoped to resettle eight Katrina families. I invited anyone interested in helping to a meeting at Lazarus House the following Saturday morning for the purpose of organizing the effort.

At the meeting on Saturday about ten different churches were represented. I explained that these families would need a place to live, household goods, clothing, transportation, and help getting acclimated to the community and finding employment. The children would need to be enrolled in school. I suggested ways that providing these services could be easily organized through their church's resources based on my experience with the Vietnamese refugees. All of the churches agreed to help. Some of them were able to assume the responsibility for an entire family, and a couple smaller ones banded together to help a family. At the end of the meeting, all eight families had sponsors.

On Sunday, these churches brought this idea to their congregations, and by the end of the week, everyone had assembled everything needed to give our Katrina families new homes. God's people can be extravagant in their generosity, much like the Lord is extravagant in the blessings he lavishes on us.

Another person from the Katrina-stricken area came to us via the hospital. She had been living in a subsidized senior's apartment, and the building was flattened in the storm. She packed up the few things she could salvage into her really old car and began driving north. She had about $200 and the memory of some friends who lived in our community. She hadn't been in touch with them in a while and when she got to our community, she was unable to locate them. She was running out of money so she was sleeping in her car to save money. Her health began to suffer and she ended up at the hospital's emergency room. As soon as the hospital staff heard her story, they contacted us. I drove over immediately and invited her to come stay with us.

Katrina victims were given priority status for housing, and so this person's name was put at the top of the list for the subsidized seniors' apartment building in our community. Within two months, they were able to move into their new home, which was furnished with generous donations from the community.

I would like to tell you that our Katrina families lived happily ever after, but that would not be the truth. They worked hard, and they tried to adjust, but they were not accustomed to living in our climate, and our cultures were very different as well.

As things began to return to a state of something resembling normalcy after a couple of years, one by one our families began to move back south. I could certainly understand their decision, and suspected that if our Vietnamese friends had been able to safely return to their country of origin, they might have returned there, as well.

To this day, I am thankful for the part God allowed us to play in helping our Katrina friends. We were able to provide love, food, housing, clothing, household goods, and hospitality at a time when they had nothing. When they returned to their community in the south, I suspect they did so with an expanded understanding of how much God loved them. My experience with them certainly expanded my understanding of God's love as well. He would never abandon his people in a convention center, and when circumstances conspired to have that happen, he made sure that they were rescued. That's how much he loves us all.

CHAPTER 17

TURNING POINT

Lazarus House had been a dream come true for thirteen years—so many changes and so many blessings, not the least of which involved my husband. Sam had been a stalwart supporter from the beginning, not complaining about all the crazy hours I worked or the fact that Lazarus House inhabited every corner of our life. Sam's health was getting worse, and in 1998, he had both his knees replaced. Arthritis and years of running up and down those aerial ladders as a firefighter had taken their toll. He recovered from the surgery, but it was a tough recovery. He had a sense that he needed to consider slowing down.

In 2002, Sam retired from his job at our city, and the next day, he came to work at Lazarus House. He was cute and willing, and he worked cheap, so we were really happy to have him. The first Monday he was with us he expressed a concern that we were almost out of milk. He knew "our children" would be home from school soon, and he thought it important that they have milk. He asked me if I thought he should get some. I told him he should do what he thought was best. With that, he disappeared out the door en route to the convenience store three blocks away.

He returned in about ten minutes with three gallons of milk. When he came up the stairs, he saw four gallons of milk sitting on the counter in our dining area. He asked me who brought them, and I told him I didn't know, that someone had rung the doorbell about five minutes ago and handed me the milk. I thanked the person, who left without another word. I had no idea who it was. Sam put the milk he had purchased in the refrigerator without saying another word. However, in future, if we were running short of any essential, he would tell me he wondered who was bringing it and what time it would arrive, and it always did.

Sam knew "Ken" well. He had grown up down the block from us and went to school with my daughters. Life was difficult for "Ken" and, through no fault of his own, he had difficulty holding a job and eventually ended up at Lazarus House. We were glad to have him. We did all we could to help him and encouraged him to apply for Social Security disability. "Ken" said he wasn't ready for that and felt he could work and support himself. We had serious doubts that he ever could be entirely self-supporting, but respected his right to choose and applauded his commitment to a work ethic.

"Ken" had a job cleaning tables at a restaurant. It was early October and as happens in northern climates, it got cold overnight. "Ken" came to me in the morning asking if we had a coat he could use. He had a long walk to work, and he didn't have a coat. Homeless people often have few possessions and cannot store things from one season to the next, so every year when it gets cold, it's a scramble to make sure our guests have warm clothing. As this was the first cold day of the year, and the cold snap was a surprise to even the weather forecasters, it caught us all unaware. I really didn't think we had anything that was suitable for "Ken," but I began a frantic search, all the time praying and begging God to provide a coat for "Ken." I figured, as long as I was asking, I might as well ask for a really big favor, so I also asked that God would be sure "Ken" knew the coat was from him.

In the middle of my frantic search, the doorbell rang. I ran down to answer the door (we always kept it locked for everyone's safety) and found a man standing on our doorstep holding a dry cleaning bag that contained a winter coat. The man sheepishly handed me the coat, telling me he wasn't sure why he was doing this, but "something" just told him he should drop this off this morning. I told him that the "something" was God, and that a man was upstairs right now who needed a coat so he wouldn't be cold on his long walk to work. The man wanted to know how I knew the coat would fit this man, and I told him I knew it would be perfect, because God sent it.

This man couldn't run away fast enough, probably convinced that he had encountered a genuine lunatic. And I guess in a way he was right; I am crazy about Jesus! I went running up the stairs and will never forget the look on "Ken's" face when he saw me with the coat. He wanted to know where it came from, and I told him that his best friend, Jesus, had someone drop it off. "Ken" tried on the coat, and it was a perfect fit. No surprise there. "Ken" may always have some struggles, but he knows that he has a God who loves him so much that he sent him a coat on a cold day.

Sam was a special friend to so many of our guests. With his quiet and gentle manner, he made people feel loved and wanted. He had a special place in his heart for our children, and it was one of them that had a role in Sam's accident.

One of our families had a teen that was diagnosed with bipolar disorder. We were able to access care for the person, but it is very hard to get medication properly dosed for teens. Their hormones are running rampant, and they hit growth spurts. Just when you think you've got their meds figured out, they grow two inches, and everything goes haywire. As a result, our young friend was going through a very manic phase. The teen had been in an upstairs room we built as an addition to the women's center so people could get after-school help with homework. We had several tutors who came by every weekday to help any of our students who requested help. The teen was running down a steep flight of stairs (someone in a manic phase may find it hard to just walk anywhere), and was literally taking the stairs three at a time and bouncing off the walls.

Unfortunately, Sam was just coming up the stairs. It all happened so quickly that no one had a chance to react. They saw each other, and Sam believes they even had a second to say hello. Momentum was behind our teen friend, who was as large as an adult, and the teen ricocheted off the wall and slammed full speed into Sam, sending him airborne and out the door. He landed at the edge of the sidewalk, almost in the street. Please understand that Sam is six feet five and weighs about 250 pounds, so he sustained quite a blow. Our friend had no intention of hurting Sam and what happened was a complete accident, but Sam was badly injured.

He was unable to move, and staff called me on the intercom to tell me that he had an accident and was outside on the sidewalk. I dashed across the street as the ambulance sirens wailed in the distance. I knelt down beside him and saw that he was having trouble breathing. I immediately appealed to the help that was there with me, Jesus, and asked him to step in and hurry the paramedics. They arrived immediately, and so began a very long night at the hospital.

Sam had several broken ribs and had damaged his shoulder badly. He had no use of his left arm. I thanked God that he had a heavy parka on and had the hood up, as I believe that cushioned his skull so he didn't crack his head on the sidewalk. There's not much to be done for broken ribs, and the doctors didn't want to attempt to do anything with his shoulder until the ribs healed. They sent him home with orders to rest.

Sam has had eighteen orthopedic surgeries. To compound this, he is allergic to any meaningful painkillers. He cannot tolerate anything in the opiate family and naisads have sent him into anaphylactic shock. Jesus and topical medications are all my husband has to combat the pain he lives with daily. His pain was especially great now.

There was little I could do to improve my husband's situation. I still needed to go to work, and so every morning I would make sure he had whatever he needed for the day close at hand. It was winter, so it was gray, and he wasn't able to go outside. He spent all day home alone with our faithful dog, Lily. Pain was his constant companion, but so was Jesus.

I couldn't imagine leaving Lazarus House. I knew some day the Lord would tell me it was time, and when he did, I prayed for the grace to listen and obey. It's always best to leave the party when they are still sorry to see you go. Now, I began to realize my time at Lazarus House was coming to a close, and my focus needed to switch from caring for the homeless as my first priority to caring for my husband.

Sam's recovery was slow. As soon as his ribs healed sufficiently (that took almost two months), they addressed his shoulder problem. They did some surgery, but there wasn't much they could repair. They suggested Sam consider a shoulder replacement but didn't recommend it as an immediate option. Sam didn't want to consider it as an option at all. Over time, he regained partial use of his arm, and he decided that was good enough for him. I completely supported whatever medical decisions he wanted to make.

In considering my transition to departure, I had medical decisions to make too. I wasn't old enough to qualify for Medicare, and at that time no one was going to insure a sixty-one-year-old woman who had some health problems. I knew for practical reasons that I couldn't just leave Lazarus House, but I also knew for the good of the ministry, I had preparation work to do.

I knew Liz was the right person to step into the role of executive director, and so, wrapped in prayer, I approached her to ask if she would be willing. When God is in the middle of a situation, it comes out right, so of course she agreed.

The board was the next step in the process, and the board members agreed that Liz was the right person to step into the role of executive director. We devised a plan to quietly transition me out of Lazarus House. I didn't want a lot of hoopla and fanfare, chiefly because I didn't want anyone in the community to worry that Lazarus House would falter if I wasn't there.

I knew Lazarus House was God's House, and as long as he was honored and acknowledged there, things would go well. I also knew there would be some people who wouldn't understand or accept that, and if they learned I was leaving, they might think things would fall apart, and they would be reluctant to continue their support.

We agreed together on a plan to announce my stepping down as executive director and transitioning to a new role at Lazarus House as of the first of the year. It was also announced that Liz would step into the executive director's role. The feeling was that with me transitioning but not leaving altogether just yet, folks would have time to get used to the change, and their confidence would not falter.

After Christmas, Sam and I visited our youngest daughter, Bethany, in Florida for a month. She had moved there in 2005 when she was recruited out of graduate school to teach for Broward County. She loved the warm weather and felt she was exactly where God wanted her. We visited her every winter, enjoying the climate and the diversity in her community.

When we returned from our vacation, I began my new role in the housing subsidy department. It was a hard job! We had several housing subsidy grants, and trying to figure out which one fit which applicant the best was not easy. Just when you thought you had it figured out, some new piece of information emerged, and you had to rethink everything. It was like herding cats! My office was now located across the street from the emergency shelter in our outreach building. I tried to stay out of the emergency shelter or women's center as much as possible, keeping a low profile so Liz could settle into her new position.

I worked a thirty-hour week and, after working sixty to eighty hours per week for years, this felt like a vacation. I was able to get adequate sleep, and I began to take time to eat right and exercise more. I have struggled with my weight my whole life, and working crazy hours surrounded by scrumptious food did nothing to help the problem. Now, I had a normal schedule, brought my own healthy salad for lunch and wasn't surrounded by all the food that wasn't so healthy (but sure tasted good). The pounds began to drop off, and I was feeling better than I had in a long while. Christmas of 2011 was bittersweet, as I knew it was my last Christmas at Lazarus House. And yet, I wasn't nearly as sad as I thought I'd be. I had been called by God to do the improbable, and he had performed miracle after miracle. Now, I was being called to move on to serve in a different way. I wasn't sure what was next, but I knew for certain what I would find there: Jesus and all the blessings he was waiting to bestow.

My last day at Lazarus House was January 15, 2012. By January 20, Sam and I were in Florida, enjoying the warm weather and wondering what was next.

CHAPTER 18

RESTORATION

When we arrived in Florida, we weren't sure what God would have us do. Were we to be "snowbirds," or were we to relocate to Florida permanently? It was hard for me to leave all the ministry work I did in Illinois, and I wondered what I would do to fill the void in Florida. God didn't waste any time making his will clear: Florida was to be our new home.

We were staying with our daughter in her home, and she was a very gracious hostess. However, we knew we had to find our own place to live, especially because my daughter was engaged to a man she met at her church and would be married in June. We began our search for housing, asking God to lead us and trusting that he would.

We've always lived modestly, but many of our resources were funneled into tuition for Christian education and supporting God's work. None of the jobs we had were of the well-paying variety (storing up treasures in heaven is a much better financial plan anyway), and we knew the home we owned in Illinois would not sell for top dollar given the state of the still struggling economy. So, we began our housing search determined to find something affordable.

In Florida, manufactured homes are a good viable housing option. Some of the manufactured home communities are limited to folks who are age fifty-five and over, and that sounded like the right fit for us. We thought living close to our daughter would be smart, as we weren't going to get any younger. We began to search for housing that fit our criteria.

We must have visited at least ten communities, and many of them were very attractive, but it wasn't until we "happened" upon one between Fort Lauderdale and Miami that the Lord spoke to us. As he has every time we have purchased a home, he literally said, "This is your new home" as soon as we walked into what was to be our new kitchen door.

Our Illinois home was not sold, and the idea of owning two houses didn't seem practical, but you are either going to believe God or you're not. We put in an offer on the Florida house that day, and it was accepted. Within two weeks, our Illinois house sold. That's God for you!

We settled into our new home, grateful for the warm weather and the warm reception we got at our park. There is a pool in our park, and we began to participate in their water aerobics, which is a great way to keep in shape. One of the lessons learned from Noah's experience with the ark is to stay fit, because you never know when God is going to ask you to do something when you're really old (Genesis 6:9-22).

We made some new friends but didn't find our number one priority at first, which, of course, was a new church home. We went church shopping and found several wonderful churches. However, God didn't tell us that any of them were to be our new church home, so we kept looking.

One day, I was chatting with a lady from our park that was battling cancer. She told me she felt sad because she hadn't been able to get out, not even to go to church. However, she said her church never forgot about her. They sent her cards and telephoned regularly. Some people would stop by to visit and bring food. She had a Stephen minister who was faithful to be there for her every week, and if she needed a ride or any other help, she knew she could call her church and they would show up. That Sunday, we went to her church and immediately knew this was where God wanted us.

We were retired, but no one ever retires from serving the Lord. We learned that this church prepares, delivers, and serves a meal for homeless folks every Monday. They also had a jail ministry and were looking at hosting a homeless shelter at the church on a rotating basis. Let me see, who do you think they could recruit to head up that effort? And just like that, God restored all the ministry work I was so worried I might miss.

Sam and I are at "Dine with Jesus" every Monday, and gladly transport and serve all the food that our church prepares to serve 150 or so people every week. Once a month I go to the county jail and facilitate a group with women, sharing my faith and God's love. Two or three times a year, I head up "shelter week" at our church. A large fellowship hall is transformed into a home for women and children who don't have a home of their own and are awaiting placement in a shelter.

The shelter situation in south Florida is not at all what I am accustomed to. Many people come to south Florida from all over the nation, reasoning that if they have to be homeless, they might as well go somewhere where it's warm. I can understand their thinking, but the plain truth is that no community can be responsible for providing services for the homeless population of greater North America.

At Lazarus House, we had strict criteria that we applied fairly, which limited our services to those who did have a connection to the community (previous address, current employment, close relative). If people did not have a community connection and they came in peace, we would certainly take them in temporarily, meet their immediate needs for food and shelter, and try to help them return to the community from whence they came, encouraging them to seek the help they needed there. We knew that we could not access any community-based services for someone who was not from our community, so there was little we could do to provide the kind of real help that addressed root issues.

Florida is overrun (as are all warm weather states) with folks who come here because they think life will be better. That's just fine when you are able to support yourself, but if you aren't, the state of Florida can't be expected to provide services for everyone. Because Florida is overwhelmed, its shelters have waiting lists.

At Lazarus House, anyone could ring the doorbell at any time of the day or night, and someone would answer the door and welcome him or her, as long as the person came in peace. If you lose your housing in south Florida, you are encouraged to call 211 and begin an intake process. The process can be lengthy, and there is no quick access to shelter. If you don't have transportation or access to a cell phone, it is very difficult to stay in touch and follow up, so you may never get into the system.

This has been a difficult reality for me to live with, but I understand its genesis. I am also resigned to the fact that I cannot solve all the problems, so I should earnestly pray and ask for God's intervention. I should also do what I can, where I am, with what I have.

God provided restoration in another area of my life too. In addition to restoring me to better health (sunshine, regular exercise, and healthy food can do wonders) and restoring my ministry work, he also restored my family.

I was adopted from an orphanage, and I knew nothing about my birth family. I didn't mourn that fact very much; I knew who I was because I knew *whose* I was. I did wish for better medical information, not just for me, but for my children and grandchildren. I have an autoimmune arthritic disorder that went undiagnosed for years. The research that had primarily been done on this condition was conducted on men in the military, so one of the conclusions of this research was that only men were afflicted with this condition. As a result, no one considered this condition as a possible explanation for my health issues.

When I was in my twenties, I went all the way to Mayo Clinic, and still there was no real help. I gave up and decided I would simply need to rely on the Lord daily to help me cope. It wasn't until my oldest daughter was twelve and began to develop some unusual health problems that both she and I were diagnosed. Not having family medical information can pose serious problems. The adoption laws were changed in Illinois, and it became possible for me to get a copy of my real birth certificate. I applied for one the very first day it was legal to do so, and it arrived two days before Christmas in 2011, just as I was getting ready to retire.

I remember opening it and seeing my birth mother's name for the first time. I also saw that the space by my birth father's name on the certificate stated "name legally withheld." When they changed the law, they did all they could to contact birth parents. If the parent was still alive, he or she was given the option of whether to release his or her information. Clearly, my birth father did not want his information released. If my birth mother hadn't known who my father was or if she didn't want to put his name down on the birth certificate, the certificate would have read "unknown" next to my father's name. I was so happy that I knew my real Father was God, and that I could always count on him, no matter what.

I'm not a bad researcher, and within a few hours I located two first cousins, one male and one female, who lived in the Chicago area. Because I don't think this kind of information should be summarily dumped on anyone, I wrote a brief letter but was careful to include all pertinent facts. I also included a copy of my real birth certificate, lest these folks think I was trying to scam them.

Right after Christmas, I received a phone call from my female cousin. We learned that we had a lot in common and had probably even attended some of the same church and library events in past years. Who knew! The even bigger surprise was that my male cousin (her brother) and I had graduated high school together!

Now that's just plain off the charts! I attended a small Christian high school, and we knew everyone in our class. I could have easily ended up marrying my first cousin.

We made an agreement to meet later in the week at a restaurant and had a wonderful time. They were kind enough to bring some family pictures for me that they let me keep, and they brought something even more valuable: the information about my brother.

I did not know that I had siblings. My mother had married a man during World War II, and she had a baby with him. The child had special needs, and after the war was over, her husband came back to America but not to her. Whether he regretted his wartime marriage or decided that a child with special needs was just too much to manage, his reasons were his own. The end result was that my mother was left alone to care for a child with special needs at a time when women were not encouraged to be independent.

My mother went to work at a company in Chicago as a Dictaphone operator. It was during this time that I came along. The only piece of information my adopted mother gave me about my birth parents was that they were married, and my father was an attorney. What I now suspect was true was that my parents were married, but probably not to each other. Perhaps my father was employed at the company where my mother worked, I'll never know. When my mother told my father about me, he apparently told her she was on her own. My mother already had a child with special needs to care for, and having another child was more than she could manage, so she put me up for adoption.

A few years later, she met another man, and they married. He adopted her child with special needs, and they had two more children together, a boy and a girl. My mother apparently had a knack for picking the same guy with a different name and haircut every time, because it was learned that this husband was no Prince Charming either. In fact, he was diagnosed with a mental illness for which he was hospitalized more than once. It was eventually learned that he was abusing his stepdaughter, and he was removed from the home. My mother was alone again, so she found yet another boyfriend of the "Prince Charming" variety.

Mother became ill in November of 1963. By that time, my sister with special needs had been placed in a residential facility, and my mother and younger brother and sister were living together with my mother's boyfriend. It was discovered that the boyfriend was abusing my younger sister, and she went to live with neighbors. Mother was hospitalized, and the birth father reappeared to care for my brother. My brother stayed with him until mother died. After her death, Social Services found out that the birth father was caring for my brother, and placed my brother and younger sister (who was still living with neighbors) in foster care.

My brother says his first foster home was a nightmare, but the second one was wonderful. He hoped he would live there until he was at least one hundred years old. He didn't get the chance because his birth father came to get him for a "visit." The birth father took both his son and daughter out of state and never returned them. My brother relates that his life for the next five years was difficult and that at the age of nineteen, he left home and never went back. His father died several years ago.

I sent my brother a letter, again including a copy of my real birth certificate. Just a very few days later, I got a phone call, and we began to tenuously see if there was a way we might be able to form a relationship. He invited me to visit him that year and attend his family reunion. The foster home he had so loved had been home to many, many children over the years. His foster parents were quite well off, and rather than using their resources to buy yachts and polo ponies, they purchased a very large house with lots of bedrooms, and they took in foster kids. Every year, these foster kids (now adults) had a reunion in a park across the street from the house in which they grew up, and my brother invited me to meet him and attend this reunion with him. I gladly accepted the invitation.

Brother Bill and I at his family reunion

I enjoyed meeting my brother and his family. My brother and I don't look anything alike, but that's a good thing, as he is bald, six feet two, and weighs about 250 pounds. We are, however, very much alike, having the same strange sense of humor and liking many of the same things. We are very close now, in touch via e-mail or on the phone, and we see each other at least annually. Restoration, that's what God has done for me in my "old age."

My older sister with special needs died several years ago. I learned that she married a man with special needs who had lived in the residential facility with her. I have pictures of their wedding and my grandmother is in them, smiling and happy. She is also hunched over, as it seems my grandmother had a bad back, the genesis of which was never determined. That certainly explains a lot about my health issues, and also explains why one of my daughters seems to have the same issues too.

My younger sister lives on the East Coast and is not in touch with my brother. She hasn't yet responded to my letters either. All I have is a confirmed post office box for her. I've decided to just send her my Christmas letter (which is newsy and always includes pictures of our adventures during the year, usually with me wearing a flamingo hat) and an annual birthday card. I hope one day my sister will contact me, but if she doesn't, I will love her just the same.

My adopted sister and I have always been close, but especially since Lazarus House began, we saw each other only a few times a year, primarily on holidays. She had moved to a town about ninety minutes away, and between that and my demanding work schedule, it was difficult to find time.

My sister sold her home in Illinois and came to Florida for a visit about two years ago. She loved it! In fact, she loved it so much that she bought a house across the street from us. Now, not only was my birth family restored, but my adopted sister was too.

Since moving to Florida, I feel especially blessed. God has showered me with blessings throughout my life, and sending me to Florida was one of his best. Every day, I wake up feeling like I did when I was nine years old and on summer vacation. Each day is rife with possibilities, and I just can't wait to see what adventure God has in store for me.

Sam and I will soon celebrate our fiftieth anniversary. He has been such a blessing in my life, and I thank God for him. Our daughters have grown into strong, faithful women of God. We are blessed to have our youngest daughter and her husband living nearby. My daughter teaches teachers, and her husband has a large, loving Italian family that has adopted us as though we've been part of their lives forever. Family gatherings are large and noisy and wonderful.

Our oldest daughter and her husband and their boys still live in the Chicago area, the only less-than-perfect part of our Florida story. But they visit us each summer, and we try to get back to see them every fall. Our daughter is a social worker at a school, and the boys are growing into fine young Christian men. Their father is a great role model for them, and that's because he too knows who his Father is.

As I look back over my life, I realize how God's hand was upon it every minute. He used everything for good, even the things that didn't seem very good at the time. Throughout my life, he was getting me ready, step by step, to do something that I was totally incapable of doing. I'm getting a little too old to work eighteen-hour days any more, but that doesn't mean God still won't have things for me to do every day. I get up every morning, thank him for the day, and report for duty. What will he have me do for him today? What will he have you do for him today? I don't know, but I can't wait to see the next chapter. To God be the glory!

I hope this journey you took with me has been a blessing to you. I felt compelled to share my story because it's really God's story—a story of blessings and miracles with no possible explanation other than God's grace, mercy, and power. He wants to bless you every bit as much too, and he has plans for your life as well. I have no idea what those plans are, and I suspect there may be more than one. Some may be as small as going over today and knocking on the door of that crabby neighbor no one (including you) likes very much, and others may be larger. Perhaps, you are being called to a ministry through your church or in your community. God may even have a task for you that will change our country or our world. If he calls you to it, you can step out in complete confidence, not because you are able, but because he is. God doesn't love me or the community that Lazarus House serves any more than he loves you and your community.

If your community does not have a homeless shelter with ancillary services, perhaps someone needs to start one. Whenever I encounter injustice or need, I ask God why someone doesn't do something. He reminds me that I am someone, and so are you. Maybe God stands ready to raise a Lazarus for you too. May your life be a series of God-inspired adventures that will cause everyone to proclaim, "To God be the glory!"

If you'd like to follow Lazarus House or sign up to receive

its quarterly newsletter electronically, please visit the website Lazarushouseonline.com. This book may also be ordered through the website. Lazarus House is also on Facebook and Twitter @ LazarusHouseIL.

Made in the USA
Lexington, KY
22 March 2017